I Went to the Animal Fair

I Went to the Animal Fair

a journey through madness to meaning

HEATHER HARPHAM

Library of Congress Catalog Card Number:
    93-41087
ISBN 08910-97643

Cover design: Shultz Design

Harpham, Heather.
    I went to the animal fair : a journey through
madness to meaning / Heather Harpham.
        p.   cm.
    ISBN 0-89109-764-3
    1. Adult child sexual abuse victims—
United States—Psychology. 2. Adult child
sexual abuse victims—Mental health—United
States.   I. Title.
HV6570.7.H37   1993
362.7'64—dc20   93-41087
                                          CIP

Printed in the United States of America

Contents

For Michelle—
put your strange hand in mine

———

Special thanks to my stepfather,
who encouraged me to write the truth here,
regardless of embarrassment or cost to him

Preface

I wrote this book over the course of a painful year.
It is not a book about moralizing, or about right or
wrong. It is about waking up to discover what is real
and true—no matter how painful that process. It's about
breaking through layers of suffocating denial. It is about a
terrible revelation. And it is about taking God to task and
finding him true.

I Went to the Animal Fair was difficult to write for
many reasons. As Frederick Buechner puts it:

> We may tell stories about ourselves as well as
> about other people but not, for the most part, our
> real stories, not stories about what lies beneath
> all our other problems, which is the problem of
> being human, the problem of trying to hold fast
> somehow to Christ when much of the time, both
> in ourselves and in our world, it is as if Christ had
> never existed. Because all peddlers of God's word

have that in common, I think: they tell what costs them least to tell and what will gain them most; and to tell the story of who we really are, and of the battle between light and dark, between belief and unbelief, between sin and grace that is waged within us all, costs plenty and may not gain us anything, we're afraid, but an uneasy silence and a fishy stare.[1]

Note

1. Frederick Buechner, *A Room Called Remember* (New York: Harper and Row, 1984), page 48.

I went to the animal fair,
The birds and beasts were there.
The big baboon by the light of the moon
Was combing his auburn hair.

The monkey he got drunk.
He stepped on the elephant's trunk.
The elephant sneezed
And fell on his knees,
And that was the end of the munk,
*   the munk, the munk.*
And that was the end of the munk.

Old rhyme

Part One
HUNTING THE ORDINARY ANIMAL

1
The Roof

I WON'T TRY to tell you anything in this book. I hate to tell, I just like to talk. Besides, you can only learn from what you see for yourself, even if someone might be holding up the picture from behind. In this case, that's me.

I stand behind my life, and I hold it up. All my honest and dishonest moments, which are all true. I don't jump up or down. I hold still so you can see. You can come close, or you can lay me down. But I can't move, since I'm on this page, and since I invited you.

I stand behind my life. If you want to, go ahead and stare. You do that all the while you read anyway. Maybe that's why people like to read, so they can stare like the children get to. And maybe some people want to be stared at. It makes them feel like they are there.

I stand behind my life. And if you hardly breathe like I'm hardly breathing, you might see right through to my soul. And if seeing me doesn't scare you away, you might look so long you see your own reflection. And if that still doesn't scare you away, you're very brave or else we already know each other.

———

I am small and weak. I wear black jeans and a black T-shirt. I like black. I have thin bony arms today. White skin. I look as small and weak and frail as I feel.

When you write a book, they tell you not to act like you are there. Stay out of it, they say. But I think that's a lie. Of course I am writing this book. And you are reading it. So why should we ignore each other?

I will even go so far as to tell you why I'm writing this book. To make sense of my life. I arrange the words and scenes and things that happen to me. I color them just so, and I'm careful to stay inside the lines. And all the while I write I cry out, Aha! Aha!

———

I could explain what happened lots of ways. Part of me wants to tell you I got eaten alive by an ordinary animal. But then children always exaggerate. The truth is I spent many years in the bottom of a sleeping bag zipped all the way shut.

I figure I'd better tell you that right off. In case you don't like the sound of it. I'm sure you're familiar with the sound of a metal zipper. Zzzziiiip. Anyone who has ever gone camping with a sleeping bag can easily hear that same sound in their mind at any time.

Except that's not what I heard. It's different when you're little and it's being shut one tiny metal tooth at a time. It sounds exactly like nothing. Click. Did she hear? No. One week later. Click. Did she hear? And before you know it, you can't feel your life.

When people are let out they go a bit mad at first. Like blind people who see for the first time. Or like someone who's never smelled anything waking up to the smell of bacon. Or like dogs with distemper or sickness, they keep trying to retreat back into the bag.

―――――

You're probably wondering who or what unzipped my bag. It's hard to say. But my first memory since being awake is that of a handsome man with dark hair. He didn't do anything except see me. I hadn't been seen since I can remember. It was a terrible shock. The glare, the light, the sun. Horrible.

I look down at myself to see what he saw, but I'm still having trouble adjusting my eyes. I notice my husband lying motionless next to me. I shiver. I try to shake him when I can.

―――――

I had a strange dream the other morning. There was an orange-haired man with an orange beard and mustache. He'd been in an accident, a terrible fall from a high place. Others had fallen with him, too, and died. He alone survived. He had suffered through months of surgeries and therapy. But now here he was, whole again.

I didn't see all this in the dream, I just knew it, the way you know things in a dream. In the dream I was sitting at a roof-top restaurant, sky above, with someone, I don't know who. This man was there, too, at another table.

Some kind of mechanical arm rotated overhead, round and round. A ride perhaps? It seemed that way. Then the person sitting across from me said calmly, Watch this. Watch what that guy over there is going to do.

I watched. The man with the orange hair reached up and grabbed hold of the arm as it swung by overhead. On purpose. He planned to. When it swung out over the edge of the building, he let go. He screamed and screamed all the way down, a man's scream, hoarse and strong and terrified. I woke up with it in my head.

The weirdness of the dream, the part I can't describe, is that I understood why he did it. Even with this man's terror floating back up to me, it made more sense than most waking things do. Why he would need to throw himself to the cement again and splatter his life once and for all.

But the part that has me hiding from it, the most horrible part, was the hollering. He changed his mind and I knew it. It was that kind of hollering. He'd have given anything not to have let go.

―――

After I was fully awake, I still couldn't make full sense of the dream, except to think it reminded me of my father.

When he was in his twenties, he got depressed and went to a psychiatrist. The doctor gave him shock treatments and put him on amphetamines. He got addicted to the pills and spent years and years trying to fight back the madness that took over.

Once, he got better for a little while. But the wounds, wounds from something—from being alive in this world and thinking too much about it—seeped and seeped. In the end, his own self drove him back up to the roof.

When my father was forty-seven and I was twenty-three, he went into the bathroom and searched for something deadly in the medicine cabinet. He took a bottle of anti-depressants into his hand, I can see him do it, and he swallowed them all.

―――

When I was twelve I went into the bathroom and searched for something deadly in the medicine cabinet. I found a bottle

18

that said not to exceed one pill every twenty-four hours. That seemed good to me and so I took them all. Then I went in my bedroom and lay down and waited to die.

———

But the drugs had a delayed effect. My dad took them before bed. In the morning he got up and walked down to the store and bought a paper and a cup of coffee. He seemed his usual self to the band of misfits and drug addicts he was living with in a halfway house at the time. They told me he was cheerful almost.

And I have always wondered if he thought it hadn't worked. Did he wake up feeling better and thinking that it was a bad day yesterday and being relieved not to be dead?

———

I waited to die. I lay on my bed and stared at my ceiling. White, meaningless, flat, ordinary. I stared at my life, my childhood. Trying to die was good, I decided. It was the strangest thing I'd ever done.

I waited to die. I stared at my hands. Now they would never get bigger. I'd never clip my nails again or dig out the dirt that got beneath them.

I waited to die. And I stared at my hands some more. Then I noticed they were mine. They looked young. They seemed too small to die. Besides, I hadn't written a note to explain.

I changed my mind. I went back to the bathroom and set the empty bottle on the counter where my mother might find it.

———

But once you jump, it is too late.

The drugs digested. They attacked my father's heart, freezing it up. He burned with fever, his head too hot to

19

even touch and he went into seizure after seizure. I'm told that as the paramedics strapped him into the stretcher, he kept saying, I'm scared, I'm so scared.

That's how I have always known he changed his mind.

And then he jumped out of the sky forever.

———

I lay on my bed and waited to die. I stared at my hands and I started to get scared. Then I heard my mother yelling hysterically from the bathroom, screaming about how someone had taken all her hormone pills.

It is hard to die.

My mother called her doctor. He said I'd be fine and he asked if I'd started my periods yet. She said no and he told her that I might. A bright spot! Some solace, I thought. But no. Nothing.

It is hard to live.

So I went to my room for four years. They say animals go away somewhere alone to die. Children go to their rooms, to grow up, or to die, depending on how you see it.

———

When my father hit the bottom, he splattered his life and the blood went everywhere and nowhere. There was none. Only his black hair laid out gently on the pillow. We all cried. He didn't leave a note.

———

Of course, other things can wake you up. It doesn't have to be knowing what can happen. It could be any shock. But I should warn you. It's hard to survive seeing. Hard to keep your hand off the zipper. And I'm still scared I will change my mind about the whole thing.

2
The Blood

I PACK MY LIFE down hard. I compact it, all the moments. Then I wait and see what rises to the surface, what is significant. I search amongst all that oozes out, all that isn't ordinary, for God.

Some days I panic, when nothing rises up and I think the ordinariness will suffocate me. On those days I'm making dinner or staring into a toilet bowl or having to stop at the store forever. I talk to people and we pass and miss and can't touch. I call someone on the phone and we have an ordinary conversation.

———

I pack my life down hard at night in my office. And then I wait, almost numb, hoping for something to break through the surface.

Last night, my period did that. It surprised me because I noticed it. Usually your period is ordinary and blood comes out every month and you plug it up and try to forget. You like it neat and clean and invisible. You

21

definitely don't clap and rejoice because you've begun to bleed.

———

My husband says my period is a good sign. He rejoices in my blood when it comes because we don't want more children right now. He's glad my womb will stay empty another month. He's glad I'm shedding that readied room, that my walls are collapsing because nothing has happened.

I wonder briefly if that's the only reason he's glad. I want to ask him what it's like not to flow blood on a regular basis. To be a man. What is it like to never wake up in your own familiar room in your own familiar blood?

———

I have an acquaintance who was pregnant recently after trying for years. She has one son who was born with a birth defect, and she's had two miscarriages since then. This time she started to spot in her third month.

She called everyone and we all prayed. I couldn't help wondering what that would be like. To be pleading with God, No, please don't let it come out. Please keep it in there. I imagined gluing it in, or pasting it, or stapling it to keep it there.

Christmas Eve it came out. She miscarried and the fetus went into the toilet. The doctors made her fish it out and take it to the hospital. I thought I would be sick.

I saw her at a party the other night. I wanted to say something. But I didn't. Nobody would let me. I could swear they all had their hands over my mouth and she had her hands over her own ears and no one was allowed to say anything. I hated it. I tried to say sorry with my eyes.

———

When you can't see yourself, it is harder, I think, to be

told good things. Harder to have someone believe in you. Because you know you can never do it. You can never be it. You crash on every step. You crash on all the words. And you start to hate the people you are going to disappoint in every imaginable way.

And so you risk. You keep standing in crowded rooms and giving yourself over to people. You hand them your innards, brown-red and coiled on the center of a dirty plate. All the women in the room keep talking about crafts and sales and their children's latest colds.

What did you expect?

You risk. You see a dark-haired man who reminds you of your father. You want him to take you on his knee and teach you and tell you it's going to be all right and that you are adorable. But he only wakes you up, says a few kind words, and then you disappear again.

You risk. You write the truth and show it to God and he's not shocked, but everyone else is. Some people are appalled and they wonder about you. You worry them. You begin to say the word *normal* too many times until it loses all meaning.

So you withdraw. You don't call a few friends for a few days because you can't pay attention to the details or pretend like you are listening. Each of your friends has a different piece of your entrails, and they think that's all there is of you, and you know they can't bear to see any more.

So you withdraw. You won't ever send out another article or piece of rot with your name and a for sale sign on it. You won't ever go up the steps again. You will just stand still, as still as possible, and wait for the war to pass and people to be looking the other way when you come out.

You come out spotted. A spotted monster. The spots are big black holes. They are like the ones in space that have no bottom. Inside them, objects spin, strange and familiar floating pieces of all the things you've used to try to plug them. The pieces drop and drop through eternity and forever.

———

Maybe some holes just empty themselves out, over and over, all your life. You crawl inside on occasion to look around, to be sure there is still no bottom. Someday, they tell you, when you're older, the holes will go away.

But whoever heard of a hole that went away?

The worst thing about holes is they have voices that cry out when you're not expecting it. You're standing there trying to smile and act mature while a little arm keeps reaching out of your words, your holes, trying to grab at a man's collar or coat-sleeves or jacket.

You don't even notice what's happening until you feel the men pull away.

———

It's 2:00 a.m. and I get up and grab my notebook. All right, now I'm angry. A writer's mind is a sick, warped, restless thing with no sympathy for the body. I lie here scribbling and frowning and finally I stomp into the bathroom and grab the over-the-counter sleep-aid pills my husband bought for me that I rarely take.

He is just getting out of the shower to go to work. He can't believe I'm still awake. He smiles at my white, haggard reflection in the mirror and shakes his head in disbelief.

I glare at him. All I need, I tell him, is a little time away from myself.

He laughs. He probably wishes it, too. You can take time away from your spouse, your kids, your friends. But you never get time away from you. And that, you suddenly realize, is why so many people go crazy.

I go back to bed and lie there with the light on and my notebook open. I think about this book and how I'm sure it's going to fall apart soon since I have no plan. But then again, it's usually the plans we make that fall apart. Maybe the thing with the best chance has no plan. A hopeful, demented thought.

I journal briefly about a friend. She told me today that her creativity is locked behind some wall. I wish I could tell her what the wall is. What is her wall? I ask God in my notebook. But even without God saying, I know my friend is insecure like me. She is trying to find her voice, always on the verge of screaming, but never speaking up.

That reminds me. I need to write a bio-note for something I wrote. I lie there and think while I'm waiting for the sleeping pill to hit. I order myself to think. Heather Harpham . . . what? This is irritating. They want me to put myself in a sentence. I should be able to do that. Okay, I could write the truth.

Heather Harpham is slowly going mad up in her den reading the journals of Sylvia Plath.

Heather Harpham hates to shave her legs in winter and looks like an ape lately.

Heather Harpham has a habit of chewing the inside of her cheeks until they are raw and scarred.

This is who I am. An identity crisis seems not so bad and almost funny at two in the morning. And now my husband comes by wrapped in his towel and reminds me to have our youngest son take all that stuff to kindergarten in the morning.

What stuff? I say.

He says our son is child of the week this week and didn't I read the notes he brought home?

What do you think I am? I ask. The kid's mother?

Then he tells me our son needs to bring a hundred of something to school today.

A hundred of what?

My husband suggests pennies. There is a jar full of them on top of the fridge, he says, and also he needs to bring ten pictures of his family.

I look at the clock and try to imagine it. In four short hours I will stumble downstairs half-dead and sort through family photos and count out one hundred pennies for kindergarten.

Don't ever stay up past 2:00 a.m. Don't ever try to be a writer. Don't let your kid go to kindergarten. Don't journal. And don't read books written by people who killed themselves at thirty.

Maybe my friend is better off behind her wall. I'm trying to smash mine down and look at me.

I talk to my journal more about this book. Don't try so hard to be logical, it says back to me. If you put two plus two together and get four you won't be writing about real life. Real life isn't logical. At its best it's meaningful. And that's what you are chasing.

———

I turn out the light and shut my eyes. But once you are awake it gets harder and harder to go back to sleep. You go crashing about your holes. You bump into yourself on occasion. Finally, you begin to bleed.

And that, you realize, is why you write. You have

26

to keep setting it out there, all of it, or you will never be able to see yourself. Besides, if you offer them a polished plate with escargot you'll only get a reward—something to shove in the hole and fish out of the toilet later.

I begin to have cramps. And that gets me going about my period again, remembering how I noticed it. In my delirious state of half-consciousness, I'm suddenly praising God. I'm glad blood is flowing out of me. Glad that my body is a violent, alive thing. Hallelujah!

Yes, maybe it will stain. But I'm glad to stain my life. I see it rise up: the evidence, the pink water, the miracle. A rose in my toilet. An apple on my bed sheets. A bright, shiny splotch on my life.

3

The Elephant

THIS MORNING MY life wouldn't start. I got my coffee and notebook and sat in my usual spot on my couch. I began the day like I always do—looking out my window at the hills. But it stuck. The day wouldn't open up or any air come in or anything. Even my mind refused to stir, no matter how much I jabbed it.

I sat there for many solid minutes. Nothing. I started to wish hard the phone would ring and I'd get interrupted by some bizarre news or invitation the way people do in movies and then suddenly everything about their life takes a drastic and wonderful turn.

My wish grew more intense until finally I began to feel that if it didn't happen, if the phone didn't ring right now, I might never recover. So I decided the phone call must be inevitable.

I tried hard to think of what the news might be. I ran the usual scenarios around in my head—I'd won a contest, money, or a trip. But none of these things excited me, and I couldn't think of a single idea that didn't sound as ordinary as that exact moment.

————

Sometimes you can't get rid of ordinary because the ordinariness is coming from inside of you. When that happens there's nothing you can do—except pray frantic prayers that the phone is really about to ring and there's something exciting but you're just not thinking of it.

————

It often hurts me to watch commercials. They fill me with longing. Even when they're trying to portray a supposedly ordinary family eating breakfast or doing laundry, they make it so you can tell this isn't really an ordinary family. There's something clean and bright and worthwhile about their lives.

The people who make these commercials know exactly what they're doing and I think it's mean.

Movies are much worse. And not just because they're often about rich or happy or beautiful people. But because they can make any ordinary person or any of their ordinary moments seem incredibly significant.

The trick is mostly the music. It's the music they play while these people are talking or running or crying that makes it seem like everything about them matters so much. I don't think it's fair, really, for them to be able to do that to us.

And I know if they played the right music every moment of my life, to dramatize it, I wouldn't live an ordinary life either. So there, I say. So there.

————

I've had two important revelations: I don't want to die until I've seen elephants mating—or at least a picture of it happening. And second, I hate men. Or at least the little girl part of me hates men.

I had these revelations the other night when my husband and I spent the evening with some friends. It wasn't an ordinary evening. We invited ourselves over and everything was spur of the moment. We ate pizza and played a game. But it was the animal talk that really saved me.

My friend told me about a cow on her grandpa's farm that went crazy when my friend was little. She said that all the other cows could sense this was no ordinary cow, and so they were cruel to her and wouldn't let her eat with them, and she finally died.

Later, when they did an autopsy and cut her stomach open, they found strange things in her innards. The lunatic cow had been eating all kinds of bizarre stuff, including barbed wire and even a pair of shoes. This cow would eat anything, poor cow.

For some reason her story reminded me of my grandma. She never ate strange things, that I know of, but she did one time go as mad as that cow. You're not allowed to get the details when you're little, because they don't think you could understand. But even without them saying, I could sense my grandma was crazy.

One night I found out for sure. I overheard my mom telling my stepdad how she had walked into my grandma's house earlier that day and found her lying stark naked on top of her Lowrey organ with all the keys blaring at once.

Now maybe you can understand why I have to worry about madness so much, seeing as how I have it coming down to me from both sides.

How our conversation got to elephants from there I

can't remember. But I'm glad it did. Because for some reason, it had never occurred to me before that elephants mate. One of those obvious but incredible facts that had managed to escape my mind.

My friend exclaimed, Oh yes, yes they do! She had seen it even, she said. I was envious and immediately I wanted to know how they can when they are so huge. How? I asked her. What do they do?

The men, I could tell, wanted us to be quiet. But we were both getting excited by now. Pretty soon, we started to laugh and squawk and wonder out loud what a male elephant's apparatus might look like. And I could tell the men really wished we wouldn't discuss such things.

But I figured that if God made elephants then why shouldn't I know all about them? Wonderful, strange horrors. What a shame if I should die without witnessing that. I'm absolutely sure that it would not, could not, be ordinary no matter what I was like on that day.

———

I think when a thing seems like it should be ordinary, but for you it isn't, you shouldn't blame yourself. The mere fact that you noticed it wasn't ordinary when it should be—that makes it absurd, and then it's not ordinary after all. And so you can feel better about it in the end.

———

I never had a grandpa. Whenever people talk about them, I can't picture or imagine what that would be like. My dad's dad died before I was born and my mom's dad hardly wanted to see her, much less me. He is alive and lives somewhere, I can't remember where. Strange to think I could see him and not know it.

I did have a stepgrandpa briefly once who I even saw

32

a couple of times. But he can't really count as a grandpa because he disliked children and he was an alcoholic and he was always falling down the basement steps. This is maybe part of what drove my grandma mad, since this was her second husband.

I also remember distinctly that he only had a few fingers on his hands as a result of some accident, which is the kind of thing that sticks out to you when you're little. The reason he was always going down to the basement was that he had an easel set up down there where he spent many hours drawing page after page of cartoons.

I thought this was strange, seeing as how he had no fingers and hated children. The cartoons almost redeemed him for me, but in the end, the hands were too much.

———

My grandma also considered herself an artist. She covered her walls with her own paintings. This struck me as vain, yet at the same time it was nice she could feel so proud. I think I finally decided it was pathetic. But I was too young to think these kinds of thoughts anyway, so I could only feel them.

One time my mother took us kids over to visit my grandma and there was a piece of toast hanging on her living room wall. Nobody wanted to notice it, but there it was, an ordinary piece of toast nailed firmly to the wall.

My mother, or else one of us rude children, finally pointed out to my grandma that she had food stuck on her wall. But it turned out she had a perfectly good reason. She said if you looked at the piece of toast very closely, you could see a man's face in it.

Sure enough, the longer I stood there and stared at

that piece of toast on the wall, the more I could see what she meant. I'm still relieved to think of it now.

———

Sometimes when you're a writer, you write something that confirms your secret suspicion that you write solely to entertain yourself. A certain thing strikes you funny. You twist around in your office chair and toss back your head and burst out laughing all alone in your office.

The teddy bears painted along your wallpaper border stare at you like they think you're strange or something. Except, of course you know they always look at you the same way, and so you're only imagining it. But at least you're having a good time.

———

Thinking about elephants made me think of Africa and I remembered the time I read in these same friends' bathroom a *National Geographic* about a tribe of people whose females wear round wooden discs in their lips.

Starting young, they make tiny slits in their bottom lips to help stretch them out to fit in the discs. As these girls get older, they keep replacing the discs with ever bigger and bigger ones. When the older women pull their discs out, their bottom lips might hang down as many as four to six inches.

Later, the article mentioned in an offhanded way that according to custom, the larger a woman's disc, the more valuable a bride she would supposedly make. So in the final analysis, she is making her lip sag for the sake of the men.

———

I forgot to explain about the other revelation, which is probably more important than the elephants. I realized that night I hated men—but now I'm not sure I really do.

Maybe it was just the talk about elephants. Maybe it's just that none of the men are my father or my grandpa.

———

This morning the phone never did ring. But I made it through anyhow. Because it finally occurred to me what the problem was: I'd simply gotten to the end of the music tape I'd been playing inside of myself, to dramatize my life.

You know how after all the songs on a tape end, there's only dead space, with a few tiny crackles and snaps. You are for those moments lost, disturbed, plummeting. But then it hits you, you silly, that the music has stopped. If you have any sense at all you go flip the tape over, so you can hear the other side.

———

I guess everyone is afraid of ordinary. And so everyone is trying to hear or see something more than what they can ordinarily see. And maybe if you don't ever let yourself get a little absurd—the absurd will get you.

Maybe one day someone will find you lying naked on top of your Lowrey organ, making music loud enough to wake the whole entire world. But at least for that one moment, your life would seem as significant as in the movies.

4
The Child

I WAKE UP LONELY. It's Saturday morning, 6:00 a.m., and I wake up in bed alone, my stomach upset. My husband must have got up early and gone to work for a few hours. Usually I wouldn't mind, but this morning I do. I make tea and toast and I try to enjoy being alone, but I can't.

That's the worst kind of aloneness, when you've lost the ability to keep even yourself company. When you're lonely like that, you might as well get mad. Get mad at your husband or God or whoever else you wish could make you not lonely. Because no one can help you.

———

I've had a dead fly on my stove for two days now. He's lying on his back, a terrible black spot. Actually, he looks like any ordinary housefly dead on top of anybody's cream-colored General Electric.

But I keep noticing him, and this morning I notice him more than anything else in the kitchen. The whole time I'm making toast and fixing my tea I see him, even when I've turned my back.

It dismays me. I want more than anything to be rid of the fly and this makes me angry at my husband. Surely he must have seen this dead bug on its back on our stove. So why won't he get rid of it? What is he so scared of?

I hate to touch anything dead, or to kill a bug that isn't. First, you get some toilet paper (I'm not the type to have tissue) and scrunch it up, but not too tight. It's always terrible, that moment you go for it. You try to swipe so fast your mind won't know what happened. You try not to look—for goodness' sake, never look.

And then you toss it in the toilet and flush it down quickly. It bothers me to put it in the garbage. Because then it's still there and you might think about it or see it again.

It's not so bad if the bug or spider or fly is already in the sink or the bathtub. Then you're lucky. You don't have to squash it, unless you want to. You can just turn on the tap and aim the water in its path and swoosh it down the drain.

Oh, you still feel that sick little shiver go through you saying that you are cruel. But you can feel more justified, and not really responsible for the bug's blood, which it doesn't have any of anyway. After all, it was crawling in your sink and all you did was the natural thing and turn on the water.

But the worst part of this morning wasn't any of this. The fly is still there. The worst part of this morning was one terrible moment when I was waiting for my toast, my back to the fly, my loneliness welling up, and I heard one of those emergency broadcast announcements come on

38

TV in the other room, interrupting my son's cartoons.

Beeeeep. Blah blah blah blah. I could just see that stupid blank striped picture they give you, and I heard a man's deep serious voice say, "This is a test of the Emergency Broadcast System. This is only a test."

And then that same constant high-pitched beep from all the emergency broadcast interruptions I have ever heard in all my life piled up into one long, torturous, hollow note that made me want to scream.

Those are the worst kinds of interruptions, the kind that interrupt your life with nothing. A dead space, a painful pause, a bald blankness. Your life keeps interrupting itself with a high-pitched note of nothing that peals inside your head and your whole being echoes with unbearable loneliness.

I guess you could say I had a bad morning.

———

Most people aren't afraid of ordinary. They can handle waking up to an ordinary morning and being alone in it. In fact, some people use the ordinary to hide from their lonesome selves. They turn on the TV or read the paper or clean the kitchen and dispose of the fly and forget they exist.

But I can't seem to find myself so that I could dispose of myself even if I wanted to. And on certain terrible mornings or nights the ordinary is like a descending pillow of space, a dull ax-blow, a shrill, protracted, silent scream that threatens to cut me off from either possibility forever.

———

I finally called my husband at work and acted cold to him because he hadn't left me a note. He wanted to know what was wrong. I wanted to tell him about the fly, and the test of the broadcast system. But I just told him I felt sick. He said he was going straight from work to play basketball. And I said, fine then, that's just fine.

He came home instead of playing and found me in my office in my sweats and my Mickey Mouse T-shirt. I was about ten years old. I was mad at him for coming home because I didn't want the guilt. We squabbled all morning. It finally blew up with him saying he hates me when I'm like this, and me agreeing.

———

This morning I didn't want to eat in the same room with the fly, so I took my tea and toast to my den. When I was twelve, my family didn't want to eat in the same room with me. Every time they did, I made someone cry. I could make them laugh, too. But there was always meanness in both.

And so it was a house rule for a while. I had to wait until everyone else was done eating, or I could take my plate into the other room. One time, I was standing in the kitchen and it was getting close to dinner and I was making them laugh. They started to put the food on the table and so I risked it. . . .

I sat down and was going to try to sit still and maybe blend in with them. But suddenly my stepdad noticed me, and then he glared at me hard and said, What do you think you're doing?

So I jumped up quickly and scurried away. It made my sister cry because she felt sorry for me, but I wanted to say, Hey, no big deal. I hate you all.

———

After a while, I felt sorry about ruining our Saturday. I went to my office and cried a lot and my husband eventually came in, grabbed my arm, and took me to our bedroom. He made me lie down, and he started to rub my back the way I like him to. After that I felt better somehow.

Maybe it was just the feeling of having someone pay close attention to me. Kind of like when you get your hair done. You sit there and go all relaxed. You shut your eyes and enjoy the fact that someone is so focused on you, even if it is only your hair she cares about.

Later, I told my husband about the fly on the stove. He claimed he hadn't seen it. We got to talking about bugs and he pointed out you shouldn't ever swoosh a live spider down the tub. How do you think it got there? he said. If they're in the sink or the bathtub, they probably crawled up the drain and will do it again.

He's right. So what you have to do is pull up the plug, hit them hard with the water until they are dead, and then let them go down the drain. If you're lucky and they're small enough, they won't get caught in the drain slots.

———

When I was thirteen, my family got rid of me for a while. They sent me to live with my real father in the Bronx in New York. I'd seen him only once since my parents' divorce when I was six.

He was living at the time in a halfway house with twenty-three other ex-drug-addicts. And there were a lot of bugs. Cockroaches. Everywhere. I remember the sound when someone saw one crawling across the hardwood floor and stepped on it. Crunch. But those people were used to that sound.

I spent my days that summer in the halfway house with a blind, black woman. She had me sit with her for hours and watch soap operas and tell her things she couldn't hear. Like whether the people were kissing or not, or if someone was glaring at someone.

She was also in charge of everyone's kids while the other adults worked. And she did most of the housecleaning and cooking. One day I walked by the stove while she was frying chicken. I looked in the pan to see several cockroaches on their backs, frying right along with our dinner.

I pointed this out to her. And she just said, Oh yeah. They likes to be behind the stove where its warm. And sometimes they gets in the pans.

My dad wanted me to stay there and go to school. But when my mother said I could come home, I did. After that, my father got depressed, went back on drugs, lost his job, and went mad for the second time.

———

This morning I wrote all the words to a song from *The Sound of Music* in my journal. It was the one about when the dog bites or the bee stings. What brought it on was I was writing about how my chocolate coffee in the morning is one of my favorite things. And the next thing you know, I felt forced to write out that whole song.

But I had to draw the line when I started to write out all the words to "Edelweiss," too. Growing up, I had a thing about that song, because it has some mysterious connection to my father. He took us to see the movie, and now a part of me can't get over it.

If that part of me had her way, she'd turn this entire book into a sentimental meandering about her childhood losses.

I guess when the man woke me up, she woke up, too. And since she won't go away, I have to be firm. But maybe I'm not giving her enough credit. Maybe it was she who woke up first. Maybe it was her crying from the crib that startled me to begin with.

I guess no one is healthy all the time. Some days you get the flu, and some days you get the little girl acting up. That is the gap you live in and it hurts some days.

———

This is all you can do: go downstairs and finally get rid of the fly, get rid of the stupid dead fly once and for all. Have no pity. Is pity the problem? Do you pity her?

But when you go down there, the fly is gone. Your husband or somebody else got to her first. You're glad for a moment. Until you notice another fly, her best friend maybe, above the kitchen sink. She's buzzing and whirring and slapping herself stupidly into the blinds.

You stand there and watch her and listen to the sound getting louder and louder by the second.

You try to remain calm. You keep telling yourself in a deep voice to remember this is only a test. It's not a real emergency. Your whole life so far has only been a test to see if you'd survive in case something ever did happen to you.

5
The Hand

MY MOTHER IS worried about her body. She called me yesterday and said she can't quit thinking about what will happen to it after she's dead. She admits this is irrational. She says she knows she'll be with God and it won't matter. But she can't quit worrying about it anyway.

I asked her if she wants to be buried or cremated. But she can't decide. I told her I don't like it that there's no grave for my father. No place to go and grieve. Only a small, silly plaque with his name on it and some ashes behind a wall.

She didn't like hearing this. She hadn't thought about it that way. I was quick to reassure her that it's no big deal and I won't be mad if she wants to be cremated. But she still can't decide which idea sounds worse. To burn or to rot. And I can't either.

———

My father always chose important days to try to kill himself. Like my sister's wedding day. Or the same day one of us had a baby. He finally did the job on Memorial Day, which makes sense. It's hard to forget dead people on that day.

It worked out better than he'd hoped, since our small neighborhood lies across the highway from a cemetery. Every year on a morning in late May I wake up and look out my bedroom window at the same scene I saw the morning he died. A hundred flags waving and flapping. And it's always the same gray, cloudy day.

———

Several weeks ago, my best friend and I walked over to that cemetery. I'd never gone there before, even though I drive by it every day. It shocked me, how many of the graves were for children. Most of them had flowers or toys on them, meaning the parents were still coming here after all these years.

One of the graves we felt drawn to was a little girl's. It was covered with pinwheels, balloons, and toys. The balloons said, I love you, and stuck out of the ground on straw legs. The pinwheels seemed out of place to me, the way they turned and flashed and smiled brightly.

I could tell some of the toys had been there a long time. A soggy pink teddy bear, a green and red Santa candle. But what I noticed right off was the doll. I figured it must have been the girl's favorite. But now the blonde hair had turned orange, her plastic face was mildewed, her skin appeared pocky and her eyes were half-crusted shut with gunk. She looked like a prop out of someone's bad dream or a horror movie.

Then I noticed the other doll and I couldn't decide which was sadder. This one was still in her cardboard box, unopened. The plastic window was fogged up and had little droplets on it. You could see the doll inside and it made it look like she was trying to breathe or something.

My friend and I decided maybe this wasn't a mother's doing. Maybe it was some poor bereaved father who didn't know better.

———

Grocery stores are scary to me. They are almost always ordinary. Nothing profound ever happens in stores and people who shop there all act ordinary, and the produce and bulk sections are the most terrifying.

The lady standing next to me scoops dried hashbrowns into a plastic bag. I look in people's carts and realize how strange we all are to one another. All these human beings come into this big building with fluorescent lights and pick food items off shelves and maneuver quietly past each other so they can eat and stay alive on the planet.

It's all so ordinary I could die. I go down the aisles sick of everything. Sick to death of food. Sometimes I stare at the red and raw meat sections, at all the dead animal bodies, and despair because I recently made everything I can think of to cook for dinner.

———

Sometimes I ask stupid questions. A certain fact strikes me as strange and so I ask. I want to know how they'll go about cremating my father's body. The funeral director gives me an irritated look. He hates to tell it.

Well, I finally demand, How do you do it? Do you just strike a match and light his sock on fire?

The director kindly explains that no, they won't just light his sock on fire. They'll strip him down and slide him into a 1,700 degree oven which will quickly reduce him to ashes.

———

Sometimes you ask a question you'd rather not know the answer to. But that's all a necessary part of it, if you want to stay awake.

———

Church is another place that can be ordinary. Sometimes I practically sprain my mind trying to imagine God is there, standing right next to me. Or on the platform. An awesome God, a consuming fire, burning me up with all of my sin.

But instead, we stand there acting like God is ordinary. And then we start to sing a song that we have sung so many times I think God himself must be ready to vomit. I imagine him crying out, No, please! I'm so sick of that one!

But I am standing there in my navy dress pants, one of them. No wonder God seems to blend in.

———

I'm learning you can't escape. There will always be people around you who are dead to you or asleep. And you have to keep moving amongst them and talking to them and trying to stay alive on the planet.

Besides, even if you started singing or screaming, making a terrible clatter, even if you started yelling stupid questions at God in the middle of the grocery or church aisles, you wouldn't raise anyone from the dead in the end, except maybe the animals.

———

My dad didn't leave anything behind but his eyes. We donated them to the Lions. Later they sent me a nice thank-you letter. But when I went to view his body after the funeral, knowing his eyes weren't there bugged me.

The mortician must have put something inside the sockets to make it appear as though my dad still had eyeballs. But you could tell by the way his lashes looked that his lids were sewn shut, stitched shut forever. Crooked even. It bothered me to think that now he could never open them again, even if he wanted to.

———

I have a writer friend whom I met during the last half hour of a writer's conference a few years ago. I said to her, You're so tall, and she said, No, you're just short, and we have been soul-friends ever since.

Because she lives in another state, I only get to see her a few times a year. But I see her more than I see most people. We run up huge phone bills tilling up each other's souls, turning them over and over and crying out in recognition.

This morning my friend saved me. It was gray, rainy. I was a little frantic, for no reason. She called me up and was just as frantic. We are both equally strange, alone, asking all the weird questions and getting weird answers.

She read to me from her journal. She was sitting there last night, she said, when she saw her hand. But this time, it didn't look like her hand. She described how the fingers appeared delicate and the skin smooth. It must be someone else's hand because it felt disconnected.

I was so relieved to hear that someone else can't recognize her own hand. It means more than that to her, of course. Usually you don't notice your hands. But then one night—there is your own marvelous, strange hand.

The same hand that looked too young to die when you were twelve.

We exclaim and interrupt each other for almost two hours. We are searching in parallel. God keeps pulling her hands off of her eyes, too. After we hang up, I'm completely cracked open. I want to jump around my office. I want to call up someone else and tell them.

And tell them what? That I'm not so mad, simply because I found someone else who's as mad as me?

Now I know if they cart me off, they'll have to find my friend, too. And if they do, we'll go wheeling toward the ward together, side by side down the hall, linking our strange hands across the parallel beds, thinking how good this is. How this isn't ordinary at all, and how we'll write about it later.

———

Sunday morning at church my husband and I ran the slide projector for the words to worship songs. We were sitting in the front row, singing with raised hands. I was trying to stay awake. Forget the ugly mole on the lady's neck at the piano. Forget the bulges in the pastor's pants from his keys. Forget—

Suddenly, flash! The light of the morning sun came through the window behind us. It lit up my husband and me and cast our shadows onto the mauve-colored altar steps. Two dark figures with hands upraised, fingers opened wide. I saw us worshiping an awesome God for the first time in months. And I could almost feel the flames.

———

I think my mother isn't really afraid of what they'll do to her body when she dies. I think she's afraid she hasn't lived yet. She's scared that hers has been an ordinary life, and that she won't wake up until it's too late.

Now she's finally ready to ask God the real questions, which are all the scary ones with missing or no answers. Questions not about what will happen to her, but about what's happened already.

—

It hurts more to stay awake. Sometimes you want to go back to sleep forever and forget what they'll do to your body. But don't you dare! If you shut your eyes long enough the ordinary animal will come along with needle and thread and sew them shut forever. Pry them open! And when the dirt begins to fall on you, when you're being buried alive by this ordinary life, don't just ask your questions. Scream them! And remember, you have at least one friend who will hear your muffled cry.

—

It would be better to burn than to rot, Mother. Beg God to light your sock on fire.

6
The Capture

SOMETIMES I FORGET I've done something right after I've done it. I'm in the shower and suddenly I can't remember if I've washed my hair or not. I go to put on deodorant and I already have it on. Where have I been? I can't recall existing in that moment.

If you miss a moment, there's nothing you can do. But if you live it, later you can toss it—if it's ordinary. If it's not, you've done a dangerous thing. Those moments stay with you forever. You remember or forget. But you can never get over them.

———

The first time my dad went mad, I was too little to remember. Either that, or I blocked it out. The second time was after I left him in the Bronx. I was fourteen when he showed up in our front yard wearing a pair of red and blue bowling shoes he'd stolen from a bowling alley. He knew he was god, and he predicted a flood to end the earth.

My mom and stepdad let him stay in our home. But he never slept. He stayed up all night. He drank coffee and went to the bathroom and went bumping and stumbling around the house, murmuring things.

In the morning we discovered he'd scrawled all over the inside of a bunch of books from the bookshelf. He marked up our ugly pea-green cloth-covered world atlas with arrows and notes and things he marked "significant." Symbols, double-meanings, signs. He was mad. Laughing mad. A generous, god-like mad.

On the third morning, I got out the Bible and showed my dad the scripture where God promised not to flood the world again. He hated me for that, I think. He didn't want me to change his mind. And he got furious because I wouldn't believe in him.

After that he demanded to be driven to downtown Seattle and dropped off so he could wander amongst his own kind, who were, he said, the least of them.

My stepdad agreed, probably relieved. I stood on the porch feeling cold and invisible and my father didn't notice me, remember me, or forget me.

Before he left, he took off his bowling shoes there on the cement steps and clapped them together, angrily, wiping the dust of me from his feet and declaring the same scripture Jesus said to his disciples. *If you go into a town . . . if they will not listen . . . shake the dust of them from your feet.*

I still choke on it. I stand on the porch and choke on the dust of his shoes, his feet, his life.

I choke and I can't forget the feeling, the fog, the ordinary yellow school bus coming to take me to school where I stared at teachers all day who imagined I'd had an ordinary morning, who had no idea what my daddy wrote in the gritty, ugly green atlas last night that I will never be able to erase all my life.

It was in ink.

———

I think I can't bear the now, the truth, the ink. But maybe I shouldn't be so frightened. Maybe I shouldn't wrestle strangers in the street, throw rocks at truths I haven't met yet. Maybe I should read the writing instead, should read what my life is writing.

———

I hear my husband upstairs a lot of dark nights dreaming. I can hear him because he stumbles around and talks in his sleep. Sometimes he does things that make me laugh.

One morning we woke up and his work shoes were on the bed and everything in the room had been cleared off the floor onto a dresser-top or shelf. He'd cleaned up in the night. He could only remember that something was crawling around on the floor and he had to get everything up high.

But other times, he scares me silly in the middle of the night. He rips all the covers off the bed, yelling frantically. Then he pounces on something only he can see. Squatting on his knees, he bunches up the covers and won't let me lift his hands to see what he's captured. To prove there's nothing there.

Usually he'll yell at me that this time he knows there's something really there! We argue back and forth, and I reason with him until, finally, he lets me peel back his hands and look under the sheets. Nothing.

The next day he tells me it was a giant, bird-like fly of some sort.

Once, he woke up cradling the light bulb from the lamp on our night stand. He'd gotten up, removed the shade, and unscrewed the bulb to take it to bed with him. I was glad it hadn't broken.

———

Tonight, I'm in my office and I hear my husband dreaming again. I feel bad. I wonder when he will stop stumbling down the hall, if he'll ever find the light, the room, the meaning he is looking for. What is he so afraid of? Or angry about?

———

My best friend and I go for a lot of walks. In spring and summer we walk almost every day, a three-mile route through a nearby neighborhood. But in winter when it isn't safe because of dark, we walk the loop instead.

The loop is the curved circular block at the center of our small neighborhood. It is possible to stay on the sidewalk and go around and around and never have to cross a street. We pass her house and my house again and again.

We also pass a house that has an automatic burglar light. When you step on a certain spot in the sidewalk, it will flash on for a moment, to alert the robber, to make him think there's someone home and hopefully change his mind about robbing you.

When my friend and I walk the loop, we set off the burglar light each time. Flash, we are lit up. Darkness. And then flash—we are lit up again. Right in the middle of a sentence usually.

I have often felt guilty we keep giving it away. How obvious to anyone watching us that the light is a silly bur- glar light. Now it wouldn't scare anyone. And the people in that house; do they get up every three minutes to see who set off their light? Of course not. They know it's us.

I keep wondering if it will ever burn out. If it does, it will be partly our fault. And if it did—would my friend and I miss it? Would we notice that the spot that used to light us up doesn't anymore?

———

One night before Christmas, I got lonely because my husband was working too many hours and we quarreled before he went to bed. He goes to bed by seven most nights and gets up for work by 1:00 a.m.

My friend I walk with called me and caught me crying and said she and her husband wanted me to come over and be with them. I told her they didn't need some lonely old housewife coming over and intruding on their night. And besides, I looked a mess with no makeup or anything.

But she talked me into it. So I pinned up my hair and grabbed my slippers, some cheese, and a bottle of wine. I pulled on my coat and trudged over there. Their house was dark, with only several candles to light it.

Their kids were in bed. We listened to music and sipped wine in the twinkling room. I don't remember a word we said. Only that I felt like a baby finally picked up after bawling for hours in her crib. You know how babies sort of gasp and heave as they try to calm down. Then they're so peaceful, abandoned.

Later, I gathered my things and started for home. I took some slides across the snowy street. Whizz. I'm Dorothy Hamill on ice. Whizz. I'm a crazy housewife. Whizz. I'm Dorothy Hamill with slippers and wine and cheese under her arm.

In my abandon, I had forgotten about the burglar light. Flash! It lit me up. And in that single startled instant I saw myself, standing alone in the street in my navy coat, my brown hair pulled up, my plain white face, my family at home in bed. I am still stunned when I think of it.

———

There are good moments and bad moments. For some reason a second, an hour, or a day sticks out of my life as significant. I keep walking around the loop, getting lit up by the yellow flash that keeps trying to give me away. I keep standing on the front porch disappearing as my father passes judgment on me.

———

This is the first year of my life, really. I'm just figuring that out. How they have all added up to this. To waking up in the dead hollow eyes of ordinary and seeing the life I've failed to live. And I begin to cry and bawl and beat my office walls with my shoes.

Life is not happening on a string strung across a room, sliding along like a clothesline. It is a piling up of moments. Moments all getting thicker and thicker. But only the ones I lived, even if I don't remember. They begin to pile up and make monstrous meaning.

———

I am my father's daughter. I write and scrawl and ramble and murmur up in my office. God will never let me see what is next. I write in the dark, blindfolded. And then I try to understand what my life is writing. Why is this thing significant or that thing?

I cannot contrive it. I try to. I delete it and I'm ashamed of myself. You can't make up your life. You can't make up moments. You can only write what is real or true. You can only write what you remember.

————

Sometimes I wish the burglar light would burn out. But I can't decide which would be worse. To have it keep flashing or to be left in total darkness. Either way, a burglar could still come.

Now that I've walked the loop, there isn't anywhere safe from the truth.

————

My friend I walk with just called to say this isn't my office. She tells me I'm really in my "den." She looked it up in Webster to be sure. She thinks she's funny. It is the lair of a wild animal, she says, a hideout, the center of secret activity, a small, squalid dwelling. They all fit! she declares.

She's right. It makes sense. This is my den, and today I'm a wild beast hunting the ordinary animal. I track him down, I sniff him out, the light flashes on and I see him. I pounce on him in the middle of the night and this time I know there's something there.

I lift the blanket to look. The burglar is wearing bowling shoes.

Part Two
TRACKING THE SUSPECTS

7
King Eglon

I AM INVESTIGATING my life. I hunt for markings, clues. I write them all down, especially the ones that lead to my father.

My mother says her first clue that he was mad was the big black vase downstairs. One day she smelled a stench coming from it. She looked and it was full of liquid. My father had been urinating in it for a month. There wasn't a bathroom downstairs and he didn't want to take the trouble to walk upstairs.

I've tried to think what my first clue was, too. But it's hard since I was so little. It might have been the time he kept us kids up all night. He made us sit on the couch and he wouldn't let any of us go to sleep because one of us had whined about not wanting to go to bed.

———

Last night I came home from some ordinary place. I glanced around the house, frantically searching for a good sign. Maybe a note on the kitchen counter would reveal a new development in my life. But everything looked normal, ordinary. Nothing had happened to me while I was gone.

I went up to my den. I could hear my two boys snoring in the next room. I plunked my purse on the floor and flipped on the light. Aha! There sat my suicidal teddy bear on the back of my couch. The same teddy bear I saw for the first time the other night, after I ripped his ear off.

I had a real rage that night. I counted it real mostly because I went somewhere else completely while I was in it. It was dark and I was curled up on the floor of my den when I came upon the stuffed bear. I used him to muffle screams that came from way back somewhere, which is how I accidentally ripped off his loose ear.

Later I started to rub the hole where the ear had been. I was done crying, heaving, settling. And so was he. I put him on the back of my couch where the street light could shine on him. I gently stroked his forehead. His hard brown eyes grew moist. I slipped my finger down his face and off the end of his nose.

Each time, it would bounce back up as he responded to my touch.

———

This is what happened to me recently. The man who woke me up sent me an article to read. It was about men and women being friends, and how we miss each other in the church because we're afraid of sex. After I read it, I realized that was part of why I'm mad at men. I can't get near any of them.

So I thought the man wanted to be my friend in this pure way. I saw how God could do something strange between us. And I imagined what it might be like. How good for me. To finally know a man, not in that way, but as a friend, a brother, or a father.

I even asked my husband's permission. And I wrote all about it in my journal. Lots of longings. But later I had to go back over every one of those places in my notebook and write with my pen at the top of each page, "FOOL! FOOL! FOOL!"

———

The man called me a few mornings later. I thanked him for the article, and then I asked him why he sent it. Did he want us to be friends like that? I won't tell you what he said. Because he talked from this side and then from that side. And you had to spot the truth swinging in between.

He doesn't see us being much better friends than we are. There is still the attraction, he points out. He can't help that he's a man. He likes me, he said, giving me a small shove, but from a safe distance.

Before we hung up, I asked him what he gets out of our friendship. He said I stimulate him. Then he laughed and added, intellectually, I mean.

———

I have a new question. Or maybe it is a new theory. I've decided there's no such thing as love. When I made the discovery, I laughed. It's so obvious. Of course there is no such thing as the kind of love I've been longing for ever since I started to have longings.

Oh, there are people laughing together. People needing each other. People making each other feel powerful or pretty. I've had those. But there's no such thing as love that is only pure love.

Maybe that's why everyone likes to imagine it so

much, talk about it, sing about it, write about it. It's real enough to make you reach for it. But your hand settles on empty air and you recoil in shock and terror. And you're embarrassed that you even tried.

―――

I have been reading the Bible. The other day I read about a man named Ehud who killed Eglon, king of Moab. Eglon was a very fat king. And Ehud was left-handed. The significance of either of those facts escapes me.

Anyway, Ehud went to pay tribute to the king. After he said flattering things to him, he pretended to leave. But then he turned back and announced he had a secret message to give the king. Eglon yelled for quiet and his attendants left him.

Ehud approached Eglon. He had a sword hidden in his sock. When they were alone, he leaned close to the king and said, God has a message for you. Then Ehud pulled the knife out of his sock and stabbed Eglon.

The event is described in detail. How the blade went all the way through. How Eglon's fat closed over it. How his flesh consumed even the knife-handle itself.

Ehud slipped away unnoticed. Eglon's servants didn't check on the king for a long time. When Eglon didn't answer his door, they assumed he was going to the bathroom. When they finally found him, the weapon was hidden neatly in his folds. You couldn't even see what had hurt him. The blood was the only clue.

―――

I've been reading books from the library. I've been noticing the marks people make. It's strange. You're reading along and suddenly you come to a sentence with a mark by it.

I stop and think, Why was this sentence so significant to that person? I read it again. It tells me a lot sometimes. The one I noticed the other night was in the book *A Room of One's Own* by Virginia Woolf.

Someone had marked the part, "Possibly when the professor insisted a little too emphatically on the inferiority of women, he was concerned not with their inferiority, but with his own superiority."

That makes me think the person who made this mark was a woman. What the author said is probably true. But I myself would never have marked it, because it's too obvious. Only an angry woman would mark that, because she enjoyed noticing this fact about the professor.

The other thing that made me think this was a woman, was the mark was only a small penciled star. But when I make a mark, it is in pen, and underlined. I feel a little guilt. It is a library book, after all.

Lately when I mark a section, I wonder if the next reader will notice. Who are we all reading these books anyway? Who are we crossing minds with unknowingly? Each of us notices the tiny marks of those who went before. We cry out in recognition, alone.

If I ever write books that make it into the library, someday I will go to some ordinary town, to their ordinary library, and see if someone has made marks in my books. And if they haven't, what then? I will be heartbroken. Or I will write better books.

———

I thought the story of King Eglon was a strange story. But today I read about Jephthah. He wanted to kill a king, too, along with all the Ammonites, his enemies. He told God that if he gave them into his hands, he would sacrifice the first thing he saw coming out of his house when he returned home.

He slaughtered his enemies. When he returned home, his daughter ran out to greet him, playing the tambourine. Jephthah was sad. But he kept his vow. First he let his daughter go to the hills with her friends to grieve and cry for two months because she would die a virgin.

I wondered why she wouldn't rather have just gotten it over with. But after two months, she came back and was willing to let her father sacrifice her. It doesn't say how. I assume he stabbed her, like they did the animals. It's amazing what a father could do to his daughter.

———

I used to cry for good reasons. Now I just cry. I lie in the dark on the floor in my living room at night and put on music and cry as if someone had died or something.

At least before I used to have pain because of this or that. But now I have pain for reasons I can't point to. Sometimes I cry so hard I have to use a towel for my nose instead of toilet paper.

Sometimes I hold my bear and we comfort each other. I try to talk him out of it. I rub the hole where his ear used to be and say, I'm so sorry about that. I tell him, I didn't mean to hurt you. I was just hurt myself.

———

The more I investigate, the more sure I am about my first clue. It was definitely the night my dad wouldn't let us go to bed. After a while, we all got tired of sitting there so long. Finally we were all crying and begging him to let us crawl back into our beds.

Maybe you never get over that feeling.

———

It's been a while since I talked to the man. But yesterday I called him up. I couldn't help it. He was glad I called, but later I realized he'd put a secret message for me in our conversation.

He was talking about his daughter. She is four. He said she is so cute. Every night she lies on the couch just before bed and says to him, Daddy, I can't walk there myself. Come get me! Sometimes he tickles her first. Then he gently carries her off to her bed.

I think he loves her.

———

I am stabbed through. Pain rapes me. I arch my back but I'm pinned to the floor. I struggle, but my arms and legs are pressed to the couch. Someone has mistaken me for a virgin. I wail and moan amongst the hills for what will never be.

Finally, I give up. I surrender. I climb up on the slab and let the pain enter. Relax, I say to my stuffed bear. Breathe deep. Jesus will put your ear back on. But as for me, I shut my eyes to avoid my father's face. My fat closes over the handle and I eat the whole knife.

8

Baby Lindbergh

IT IS MAY. I scrape the floor of my life. I try to clean it up with a spatula, but a lot of it won't come off. It's like the dead opossums all over the road this time of year. You drive by and avert your glance and try not to look.

It is May. I scrape the floor of my life. Then I put it in a tall black bucket and walk away quickly before I can see what it was.

———

I don't expect to write today. I am in mourning. Some ordinary animal has crawled inside my heart and is dying. Now and then a leg twitches. The body of it jolts—but it is dying. Unseen, all alone. And I'm glad.

———

We gave our youngest son a new puppy for his sixth birthday. This morning I took the puppy to my son's school for show-and-tell. I wore all black. It was misty, cloudy. I almost took a coat, but I wanted to feel cold.

On the way to school, the dog insisted we stop every

few steps. Each blade of grass, each pebble or piece of garbage intrigued him. I had to keep tugging him along so we wouldn't be late.

I thought my son's kindergarten class would be ordinary. But it wasn't. The kids spread out around me on the floor, their legs flung in all directions. My son was shy, but pleased and proud. His friends raised their hands with questions about the dog, and he called on the quiet ones with an innocent air of self-importance.

I sat on a too-small chair next to my son. The children grinned at me whenever I looked their way, especially the girls. They probably thought I looked like a nice mommy. And I almost felt that way, sitting there answering questions about the puppy. He will get about this big, I said. Yes, he likes to chew.

I could have sat there all day, under their admiring gaze. I could have made that kindergarten floor my home, curled up there on the rug, and let the kids pet me.

On the way out of the school, the puppy was fascinated by a large group of kids doing jumping jacks in unison on the blacktop. He jerked to a stop, went stiff, and stared. As if in disbelief. He'd never seen such a thing— of course.

Then I pulled him toward the gravel path that leads through a field to our neighborhood. Just as suddenly as he'd stopped, he decided to sprint. The dog sped unheeding past all the things that had fascinated him on the way to the school.

I ran, too, for as long as I could. I could hardly keep up. I finally dropped the leash when we neared home. But he knew right where to go. He raced for the front door and

I stumbled behind, out of breath, gasping for air, but able to breathe.

———

My youngest son's friend had a birthday, too. My son went to his party the other day. I'm not fond of children's parties, but I stayed, because the mother is a good friend, and because you never know. Maybe it wouldn't be ordinary.

Sure enough, one kid saved me. They were playing a game of pin the nose on the clown. This kid cheated. He could see through a hole in the mask. After they spun him around and around and pointed him in the right direction, he walked straight to the clown's face and pinned the nose dead center.

But the best part came later. This same kid, who I've never seen before in my life, walked right up to me and told me that he cheated at the last birthday party he went to, too. Five times! he said. I could see through the holes. And I just couldn't help myself!

How did he know he could tell me? Anyway, my friend got the whole hilarious confession on videotape.

Later at the party, the children were trying to smash the piñata. Blindfolds were again in place. I guess nothing you do as a child while you can see counts for anything. The prizes go for being blind and still managing to accomplish something.

At one point, my son hit the piñata and broke it—but only one leg flew off. And none of the candy spilled out. The kids were stunned for a second. Now what? they wanted to know.

Keep hitting it and hitting it, we grownups said. Hit it hard until it is entirely broken open and all the candy spills out.

———

I have a guitar string in my gut. But it plays words instead of music. And it's hard to get to sometimes. I have to sit very still, hardly breathing. I reach toward it gingerly with a small finger and try to pluck it. Sometimes I'm scared to. I'm afraid it might hurt. Or what it will say.

Also, it will only work if I promise to tell the truth. I have to cover my eyes and try not to know what is happening. I have to be careful and not let my mind look at what I'm saying, or it will argue or else try to lie.

———

Sometimes after I get done writing, I pull my hands from my eyes and they are shaking. Then I read my life, what I have written. I go back to the scene where my pain climaxed. And I find myself lying in a pool of urine.

I remove the knife and examine it. It belongs to the same men. I pay the detective and tell him to go away. I have found the information I needed.

———

I called my friend who can't recognize her own hand. I told her what terrible things my life has been writing. She understood, like I knew she would. I'm sorry, she said. I'm so sorry.

———

Writing is like retching. God puts his hand on your back while you hang over the toilet. There, there, he says. Is there any more?

You don't try to clean yourself up until you know you're done. Why bother? At some point growing up, you quit crying for your mother. You decided you would rather retch alone. When does that happen?

I asked my husband. He said that maybe you don't

quit crying for her—maybe she just quits coming. I laughed. Good point, I told him, good point.

———

My sister and I used to share a bedroom that had knotty-pine paneling. I always hated the eyes in the knotty pine. The twisted knots. I felt looked at all the time. But little kids like to imagine things like that. Monsters. Eyes in walls.

But then one day, I found a hole in the wall. It led to my brother's room. I told my mom and stepdad. My brother denied it. He kept saying no, no, no way. I was scared a little bit, because I believed him.

I stuffed some tissue in the hole and tried to forget it.

———

The dog likes me instead of the children. He keeps coming to my den to find me. Then he lies as close to my feet as he can get. At first, I wondered if I could write with a dog in the room, panting, watching me.

Whenever I look at him, he looks at me. What? he says. What now?

I don't know what to say back. How do you tell a dog what is happening to you?

———

One night both my boys had terrible colds. Their noses had been running and running. When my husband checked on them before we went to bed, he called me to come look. He was laughing. There the two of them lay, sleeping side by side, wads of white tissue protruding from all four nostrils.

They'd gotten out of bed and gone into the bathroom for tissue to plug them up all by themselves. It was the funniest thing I'd ever seen. Pathetic. We left them like that. We knew it'd fall out sooner or later.

———

Last week I read some of Anne Lindbergh's diaries. My husband was out of town so I took a book to bed. We'd run out of regular light bulbs. And my husband had put in a bug light bulb instead. So I read about the kidnapping of Lindbergh's baby in a bright yellow glow.

It was a library book, and I noticed the markings again. But these weren't the regular kind. In certain places where the author had recorded an assumption about the kidnapping of Charles Lindbergh Jr., someone had written in pen, "Wrong." Where she announces he is dead, someone wrote in teeny, tiny print, "He is alive."

Next to a spot where she had commented on the brutality of the kidnappers, they wrote, "Loved that Lindbergh kid." Where she reconstructed the crime and said the kidnappers handed the baby out the window in a burlap bag, the person wrote again, "Wrong."

I couldn't concentrate on what Lindbergh wrote, because the tiny pen notes here and there distracted me so much. Also, I noticed that every section in her diary was written from Hopewell, New Jersey, where we lived while I was little and while my dad went mad the first time.

I finally gave up the book and turned out the yellow light.

———

It's hard to reconstruct a crime, to tell what happened, especially when it's against a child. No one else remembers. No one else saw the baby get taken, and it was years before a man was finally convicted and executed.

There is a baby missing in my town, too. But it's ordinary. And so no one cares like they did when it was the

Lindbergh's baby. It's been missing for seven weeks. But they have no leads or clues. And personally, I'm starting to think the dad did something to it.

———

Sometimes the truth doesn't come out until much later. My brother's room used to be my stepdad's workshop. It turns out my stepdad had drilled the hole. He'd been peeking at us through it all along. He's confessed to it now. Said he just couldn't help himself.

———

I grab a bat. I swing at all the fathers. I smash what is hanging there again and again. A leg flies off. I tell myself not to look. You shouldn't see this.

I swing the bat again and again. My life begins to split up the middle. Finally I break it wide open and all the truth falls onto the floor. I fall to my knees to gather it up. The dog goes stiff and stares in disbelief.

I hang my head over the toilet and cry. But my mother never comes to save me.

9

Robert Louis Stevenson

I HAVE FOUND my life. Or at least I've found my child-hood. Last week I went to my sister's to baby-sit her kids, and there it was, sitting on the end of her coffee table. I'd forgotten it existed. The worn blue book with a picture of a girl holding a rake on the cover.

I opened *A Child's Garden of Verses* by Robert Louis Stevenson and began to read from a yellowed page, "When at home alone I sit, And am very tired of it . . ." Aha! Aha! I knew the rest from memory. "I just have to shut my eyes, To go sailing through the skies."

I must have screeched aloud, because my husband came into the room saying, What?! What?!

The book! I cried. This was my book! This was my favorite book when I was little!

I stole the book from my sister. I took it home, curled up in my den and wept when I read, "All by myself I have to go, With none to tell me what to do—All alone beside the streams, And up the mountain-side of dreams. The strangest things are there for me, Both things to eat and things to see . . ."

——

My mother had found the book in storage. She thought it was my sister's. It has her name written in it. She thought my sister would like to display it in her house because it's so old and beautiful. But when I told my sister I had stolen it from her, she said, That's okay. I guess it was always yours anyway.

——

My sister and I have been talking a lot. On the phone. Adding up clues. Trying to remember. Frantically trying not to remember. She told me she's had some flashbacks. I said, Oh, God, don't tell me. I said, It was you, you know. You were older. It happened to you more. I'm sorry, I said. I'm so sorry.

——

My sister used to want to die. In her early twenties she attempted suicide a couple of times. She spent many years in therapy. Her doctor kept saying, I think your father . . . and my sister kept saying, Absolutely not! And when my stepdad's peeping came out, we both thought, That is it! That is it!

But just last week my sister walked out of church because a man three rows in front of her was rubbing his wife's neck. She has always hated rubbing. I have always known that. You can't be too touching or affectionate around her.

——

I've had a birthday. Right in the middle of this book. This was only one year in my life. The year I was twenty-six. Now I'm twenty-seven.

My friend I walk with bought me a new copy of Stevenson's book for my birthday, because the old one was falling apart. I still love the old one. But I read from the new one.

"Whenever the moon and stars are set, Whenever the wind is high, All night long in the dark and wet, A man goes riding by. Late in the night when the fires are out, why does he gallop and gallop about?"

———

My sister and I told our mother what we suspected about our father. She acted shocked at first and said, No, no. . . . But then she admitted she's blocked out a whole year. The year when she was twenty-eight. Next year for me. She can't remember a thing, she says. Christmas or holidays or birthdays or even being alive.

It was that last bad year with your dad, she says.

My sister and I told her all our clues—and then she remembered some of her own. But she still kept saying, Oh, I hope not. Oh, I hope not!

———

I told my sister, it doesn't have to be so horrible.

———

My sister is scared. She says it's like you have this tiny corner of a blanket you can see. But that one teensy corner is all you can bear to look at. The rest of the blanket is too terrifying.

———

This book is impossible to write. I cannot write another word of it.

———

I came home last night from some ordinary place and there was a light blinking on my answering machine. A message. It was the voice of a woman I don't know. She said she hoped she had the right person. She was looking for the woman who wrote the book.

Her name is Faith, she said. And she was calling long distance from Michigan. She had to call and tell me how much my book had meant to her. You have no idea, she said. Thank you so much for writing that book. Beeeeep.

———

I'm so sorry I missed you, Faith from Michigan! I could have used a friend today. And you left no number. No address. No city or last name.

Now you will never know how it really is with me. Or how I went to sleep last night thinking, There is Faith in Michigan! There is Faith in Michigan! And I got up this morning and played you again. One more time before some ordinary message erased you forever.

———

A few days ago a man I've never seen before came into my kitchen and sat at my table. I had just wiped away all the cereal crumbs from breakfast. He turned on his tape recorder and set it down between us. Who are you? he wanted to know.

I told the reporter all the least important things. All the things I am trying to be—a wife, mother, writer. Then he asked, what happened with your father?

I was shocked. How could he ask that? How could he do that to me? But then, oh, yes, of course. I remembered. My first book was about fathers, too. I was trying to help other women.

———

Oh, Faith, I'm so sorry! Are you twenty-seven? Did your father leave you? Hurt you? Of course he did, or the book wouldn't have meant so much. I wonder about your father. Did he hit you? Touch you?

There are things I would say to you now. Things I didn't write in that book. Things I didn't know yet.

———

I saw myself once while the reporter was here. Sitting in the chair across from him with my tan legs crossed, small and self-conscious in my new white rayon shirt and dark jean shorts. Calvin Kleins even. The ordinary house-wife who wrote some small religious book, trying to look pretty for the reporter from the paper. . . .

———

My sister sucked her thumb until she was twenty-four. I sucked my thumb until I was in the third grade. I always liked my right thumb and she preferred her left. I could never understand how she could do that. Sometimes I would try to suck my left thumb just to see what it was like and I always hated it.

Each of us, my sister and I, had something we liked to feel with our free hand while we sucked the thumb on the other. I had a blanket. My sister loved crumbs, small particles on a smooth surface. If she came to your house she would put her hand under your couch cushions.

———

I read from the book almost daily. For comfort. Some-times, when I come to a picture or poem the little girl part of me especially remembers, she shrieks with joy. She loves to recall anything unique to her childhood, espe-cially when it's something innocent, simple, and lovely that the adult has overlooked.

"When children are playing alone on the green, In comes the playmate that never was seen. When children are happy and lonely and good, The Friend of the Children comes out of the wood. Nobody heard him and nobody saw, His is a picture you never could draw, But he's sure to be present, abroad or at home, When children are happy and playing alone. . . ."

———

Oh, Faith! How I would have loved to talk to you! Someday I would like to run into you. In some ordinary place. And you would say, Oh, you are her? I'm Faith from Michigan. And we would say how small the world. And how big God.

I picture you. Calling directory assistance. For what city, please? And you saying my town. And the name? And you saying my name. You are going to call up this lady you don't know. She wrote a book, so you feel like you know her.

But what would you really think if you met me? I am only an ordinary housewife. I'm just a girl. But still. You could tell me what you see in me. And I could say what good I see in you.

———

My sister called last night. She said it was hard for her to say this. She feels angry. Like I am still the special one. I was always Dad's favorite, his pet. And now, by writing about him, I've found a way to keep it that way.

She said she knows it is irrational, but she is jealous. And then she said she had a horrible thought she hated herself for having. A sick thought. What if it happened to you and not to me? she said.

———

The reporter had brooding brown eyes. He reminded me a little of the man. His voice sounded gentle and careful.

My own voice sounded rambling and wild.

I laid it all out. The holes in my heart. Everything, except what I suspect. And then he shook my hand. We touched once coming. Once going. He turned off the recorder and thanked me as he packed my pain neatly into his briefcase.

———

Oh, Faith! Where is my faith? In my marriage? In my life? In God? I missed your call because I was out to dinner. Acting ordinary. Celebrating my first royalty check. My blood money. My book is selling because there are so few fathers and so many Faiths.

Oh, Faith! You weren't sure that you had the right person. But the reporter could see it all over my face. Tell me what happened with your father, he said, as a man went galloping by.

Oh, Faith! Who is innocent here? The right thumb or the left? Tell my sister I'm sorry. The book has always belonged to me, even though she had it first.

10
Curious George

I'M AFRAID OF MY life now. What will become of me or what won't. I have seen the man again. I ran into him, on purpose, at the bookstore where he works.

We drove to another town, where there were boats and water and lights. We had to wait for a table. Stay close to me, he said. And he took my hand, my arm. You could lose your wife or girlfriend in a place like this, he said.

When we were finally seated, the man took the chair that was across from me and put it at the end of the table so he could sit closer.

———

Last week I went to a writer's conference. There were men in the class I taught. Not the man, but two older men, old enough to be my grandpas. When I saw their names on my list, I wasn't happy. But it ended up being good.

Both of the men liked me. They kept saying how

smart and helpful I was. One of them even hugged me and kissed my cheek at the end of the conference. His gray whiskers scratched. Later, it made me cry to think of his kind, gray whiskers.

―――

The man held my hand in the restaurant. And I held his. If you'd walked in and seen us you would have thought, Aha! Those two people are in love. He touched my face. One time, he reached over and stroked his finger down my arm so that I stopped talking mid-sentence.

It was all very much that way. You know the way things are when you are like that. And after a long time, we went outside and walked the dock. And he said, Let's pick out our boat. And I said, Oh, yes, let's. Where shall we live? He said, San Diego.

―――

Last week at the conference, I let a friend read some of this book. A woman I had met there last year and got to know better this year. She kept saying my life before I could. But when she came back after reading some of it, she didn't know what to say.

An old lady in my class was writing about how to keep love alive in marriage. Another woman was writing about prayer. And one of the old men was working on a book about aging. What have you been writing? they all asked me.

Just mostly my column, I said. Just mostly my column.

―――

A couple of times, in the restaurant, I thought the man looked so much like my father. Was my father. Or my brother even. And he said I looked like his sister. And I said, What about your mother? Do I look like her, too? And he laughed and said, Thank God you don't look like my mother.

———

This book is not about the man. Or my father. Or the man's mother, for that matter.

———

We talked about the ocean as we walked the dock. I told him how I used to go to the Atlantic when I was little and we lived in New Jersey. I said the waves were huge and stood straight up as they came in for you.

I remembered to myself that one time my father held my hand as we stood there, facing the foaming blue wall. And then it smashed into us, swept us up and shook us both loose from ourselves. And he let go of my hand.

———

At the end of the dock, the man and I stopped and faced each other. I was talking to him about his childhood. I might have touched his tie. I only remember that he looked at me. And the dock and the boats disappeared. The sky started teetering in the sky. Don't stand so close to me, he whispered. Don't stand so close.

Then the whole sky came down like in Henny Penny. God sucked in his breath. Eternity shook in her shoes. The dealer at heaven's table eyed both players. The stakes were high, so high, so high. . . .

I took a big step back. The moment broke. The sky shattered and fell around me in pieces on the dock. The man smiled and frowned. I was just about to kiss you, he said. I was just about.

———

Now it's been almost two months since I saw the man.

But moments with the man still haunt me. Stay close to me. Don't stand so close.

———

My friend I walk with thinks it's funny that I call the man, "the man." She has never seen him. But she says whenever I mention him, she thinks of the Man in the Yellow Hat in her children's Curious George books.

———

A few days after we went out, the man called me up. He said we couldn't be friends anymore. And that he was sorry for taking me out. Then he mailed me two letters that said that same thing. Then he called me up again after I got them. And I said, Did you change your mind?

And he said no.

———

I went outside tonight and sat in the new bench swing I bought for our deck. I curled up in it with a quilt as the sky turned deep purple around me. Or black. I swung and tried to write my life. When I stopped writing, the next thing I knew I was singing. "Away in a Manger," of all things. With tears.

I love you, Lord Jesus. Look down from the sky. And stay by my cradle 'til morning is nigh.

———

Stay close to me, don't stand so close.

———

Before I got out of the swing, I glanced up and saw the back of my house. I noticed my den light was on upstairs. I'd left the blinds open in the window. And I could see the light fixture clearly. I'd never noticed exactly what that light fixture looked like.

I thought how strange. Who is the woman who lives

in that room? She has a family. Does she love her husband? Her form will darken that window in just a few minutes. Her shadow will appear and maybe she will pause for a moment. But no one will notice.

———

"All round the house is the jet-black night; It stares through the window-pane; It crawls in the corners, hiding from the light, And it moves with the moving flame." R. L. S.

———

I taught a lab on journaling at the conference last week. I said to them, Write it down. Write it all down. What hurt you today? Or didn't? What moment should have been ordinary, but wasn't?

You have to believe in your life, I said. You have to move closer to your life before you can move the reader closer to hers. You must take hold of your pain. You must become convinced your life is profound.

A few of them nodded in understanding. The rest of them would never notice themselves or the absence of themselves in their own window. And you could tell they were the happiest ones by far.

———

I told my friend I walk with that the sky keeps falling. The sky keeps falling! I said.

She said, You have to want God more than the man. And I said, Yes, I guess so, even though I couldn't feel the difference.

———

Once my friend I walk with wanted to love another man, too. And I helped her through it. We walked miles and miles before she was better. She couldn't get over it. Now we go sit in the back yard in the dusk after we've walked our route and I ask, Why did I step back?

My friend and I stay out on the lawn until almost dark. She's trying to help me through it. We feel the green grass prickle our bare legs. Her dark eyes flash while she talks, and I hope it is working.

———

Sometimes I scare myself. The way I start writing other people's books, their lives, in my mind. They're talking to me and all the while I'm putting it in paragraphs with hiatuses. I start to see chapters. I spot symbols and want to cry out, Aha! Aha!

But you can't put it all in. I have written ten books to write this book. At least. This chapter used to be about something else altogether. But what is false starts falling off after a while. And so I delete my life, what happened that seemed so significant but doesn't belong.

———

Not everything in life that is true or good belongs.

What should I tell you about the man? You are probably curious, like George. The man is every man. He is the Man in the Yellow Hat. He is every man who loves God, and every man who doesn't. He is every man whose mother left behind holes.

———

At bedtime, my friend's children get in their jammies and climb on her lap with toothpaste on their innocent lips and a book in their hands. What mess did Curious George manage to get into this time? Her children smile and wait for her to turn the next page. They're hoping it will come out all right.

———

I come in the house and climb the stairs to my office. I

pause in the window just before I shut the blinds. I see my neighborhood outlined in the dark: the home of the friend I walk with, and the house with the burglar light. Then I see a woman standing in the street wearing a navy coat with slippers under her arm.

I'm about to yank the blinds shut when I notice that same woman outside on the deck in the swing. She is singing stay by my cradle 'til morning is nigh. And she's thinking about the man with the gray whiskers, not the Man in the Yellow Hat.

Then she looks up and sees me and I see her.

11
Aslan

I TRAVEL TOWARD my life. And I hear it growing louder. I don't know where it's headed, but it feels like a freight train departing, going somewhere. As if it has a destination. And so I begin to write as if I'm convinced it does—all the while secretly bracing myself for a crash.

But you can't let the other passengers, or more importantly, the train itself, sense your fear.

Trains mean something to me. They make me think of my mother singing that sad song about missing the train she's on and hearing the whistle blow and knowing she's gone.

She went through a guitar phase after she left my dad gone mad back in New Jersey and she sang that song to us kids. She must have been lonely. I was six when we left on that same train and went to Washington and stayed with her mother, the grandma who nailed toast to the wall.

She sang other songs, too, ones like "Kum-Ba-Yah." Now I think, How sad for her. And how of course trains will always remind me not of my mother, but deeper, of losing my father. And of my sister throwing up in a garbage can at the terminal. Of feeling alone, lost, barely connected to my weary, small life.

It was a five-day trip, and at one stop I vaguely recall my mom begging the train people for a place for us to rest, and being led to a tiny white room where they had first aid and all of us lay down on little white cots.

———

Trains are sad things. The look of them. The sound of them even. It's as if someone figured out the exact sound of leaving, pulled it out of the universe, and made a train to match. And it just so happened to be a vehicle that could also do the job, could take people away from each other.

Airports. Now there's a different story. Yes, there are departures on planes, too. But they bring more to my mind the idea of reunions. I think of happy, tear-streaked faces and hugs and people crying out in recognition when they see their person walking up the ramp.

I think that way, even though it wasn't that way for me. When I went to stay with my dad in the Bronx when I was thirteen, I got lost at Kennedy International Airport. I couldn't find him and I kept walking through the crowds, looking. . . .

Then an announcement came for me to meet my father at the phone booths. And then I remember I was checking all of them, gazing across the row of people's backs, searching for a dark-haired man who could be my father.

After I found him, after the airport, he took me to a Chinese restaurant for lunch. The waitress thought I was eighteen or something. She asked if I wanted a cocktail before my dinner. Then on to the house in the Bronx.

———

I am still thinking about the man too much. The dark hair, the sharp blue eyes, the tall frame, the intellect. No wonder all the sameness. The man is like me because he is like my father and I am like my father, except that I am not tall.

My sister is like my mother. My mother stops by while on vacation to see me and stays one night, and then she is almost anxious to go, and I am almost anxious for her to be gone. But she stays at my sister's for several days. They garage sale, sew, and do all kinds of things that would make me crazy.

———

I went to the beach for a whole day last week with an older woman, a writing friend. She is not motherish. But she is mentorish. Wise. And slightly terrifying to me because she knows exactly who she is. And because her eyes can see right through me.

I was determined not to say a word. About my father. About my struggle. But she was like a lion next to me in my van. Not voracious. But like Aslan.

I blabbed my pain. I said I can't get over it. The man. That I can't have him. It's ridiculous, isn't it? That void. That void. That hole. He has walked away. But I can't seem to. I don't want to walk away. I am trying to walk away.

She said nothing and everything. We watched the gulls. We rented a room and I read her stuff and she read mine. We sipped wine after lunch. Then we read each other's poetry aloud and propped up on pillows and watched the men go by.

Two men. Two ridiculous men were mowing the lawn directly outside our sliding door. And weedeating! BZZZZZZZZZZZZZZ. I called the desk twice. Get these men out of here! A maid came and said something to the men once.

After that, they got more determined. They set about mowing the strip of lawn right in front of our door, over and over, until we thought there couldn't be any grass left. Until finally my friend said, Oh, good grief! He's going to mow the sand!

And he did, as soon as he ran out of lawn. It took them hours. All day they mowed and weedeated in front of our window. When the men finally went away, the silence ruined us. So distracting.

We gave up and walked the wet beach. And she said, It's okay that you can't get over it. Maybe you never will. Maybe that hole will never fill. She said, Maybe your learning to leave it empty is the meaning of your life.

———

My favorite times of writing involve no writing at all. I am not constructing. I am not planning. All my effort is in hearing, feeling, listening to that train, and then letting it plow right through my chest.

I sense that if I falter, if I'm false, if I betray myself— it will derail. Like the Amtrak train in California last week, that killed eleven people. That could happen to me. That could happen to this book.

———

My father never sleepwalked in the Bronx. Another damning clue. My mother told me she'd let me know if anything else came to mind. But this came to my stepdad's mind. When my mom told him what we girls suspected, he immediately said, Well, of course, and reminded her of something she'd told him years ago.

How my dad used to sleepwalk. How he used to come upstairs and get into bed with us girls sometimes. And we would come tell her, Last night Daddy got in bed with us. How he even fell down the stairs once in the middle of the night doing that and broke his leg.

I know now why this stuck in my stepdad's mind. And I know, too, that people don't usually sleepwalk where they're not used to being. And all the way upstairs? When he was too lazy to go up the stairs from his den to go to the bathroom?

———

I sat just now reading and flipping through poems. I keep books in each of our three bathrooms. And then when the time comes, I try to decide: Do I want to read poetry in the boys' bath? Or Dillard in my own? Or do I want to get some spiritual guidance from Merton downstairs?

I chose poetry just now and read one of my favorites, the "Elder Sister." It is about how the sister went out first, protecting the younger. But it is written with such pith, such cruel feeling, I enter every word. And I am revived.

I could live this way—off thoughts and musings and reading and writing. I could chew the paper, I think. And drink ink. And let this small den swallow me in the end. And then God would swallow it. Like the horse that ate the fly. . . .

———

I woke up this morning feeling dead. Last night I'd been congratulating myself in my journal for how I've been forgetting the man. So of course I went to bed and couldn't sleep for thoughts of him.

But then I took my shower this morning. I got my coffee and came into my den. And as I drank it, I could feel the morning, or someone, or God trying to soothe me. Trying to make peace with me. Even the cloud cover outside my window felt like a balm, like God himself holding his hand in front of the rays.

I took a huge swig of coffee. It tasted particularly good and I felt the hotness of it going down my throat into my empty stomach.

———

I admit it—my life is wrapped around him still. That I can't quite get over it. That particular loss.

———

Life itself must be about loss. A loss we cannot, any of us, quite get over. Maybe it is God's loss. Like there is a day Jesus died inside each of us or something.

———

My friend who is like a lion is sixty. I told her I don't like knowing someone that old. She could die, I pointed out. I could lose her, too. But she just laughed at me. She said she doesn't plan on dying at all.

When I call my friend like a lion on the phone, she knows my voice. So I always just say, Hi, it's me. She's made a joke of it now and she answers, Oh, hi, Me. This is I. Then a few days ago she called and said, Do you realize that we are we?

———

My friend like a lion means something to me.

———

It's strange that you can come to know someone better even after they are dead. My father's yellowed fingers cannot shake now. He can't gulp his coffee too loudly or brush back his black hair with his nervous hand or smoke or drink or think too much.

But he is still here. In spite of time. In spite of ashes. He haunts my life. He is my father.

———

At the beach, I told my friend like a lion all about my night out with the man. What happened and didn't happen. How I am hurting. I felt fine the whole time I explained it. This man and I went out. He apologized. Now we're just friends.

But then I knew for sure this was really about my father. I knew for sure because I didn't mention my father in any of it and yet. . . .

When she suddenly said to me, Heather, don't you know that whoever this man is, he can never replace your father?

I choked. My mouth tightened in pain. My eyes barreled into the sand. Don't say that! I wanted to say. Don't say that! But I held on somehow until the train had passed all the way through. I let go of my father's hand. And then it was gone.

12
Moses

OUR FAMILY IS CAMPING. I take a shower after dinner in a small wooden stall. I put on my jeans and a favorite black sweatshirt. I feel like me. I grab my journal and a cold Coke out of the ice chest. I ask my son and his friend to walk to the playground with me.

When we get there, I plop down against a large stump. Then I look up—and I'm shocked. This is no ordinary camp playground! It looks gothic in the dusk. The equipment is a wooden fortress with slides on either end. A gangplank arches over the top with swings hanging below. It sits on the edge of a lake against a pink sky with purple clouds.

And my son is a knight. My youngest son is a black silhouette walking across the bridge. He stops, his back to me, and seems to stare out over the water. He is six. Then his friend's black form walks out to meet him and the two of them confer.

It is that Hour. That hour just before dark that can

heal almost anything, whatever it is, that hurt you today. Sensing this, many children have converged on the fort. They play together, but apart. They are mostly strangers, having only this in common—our parents brought us here to camp, and yours did, too.

Most of them will forget this—each other and this exact moment—as soon as they climb in their bag. Only the lady, or is she just a girl? Sitting over there with the notebook. She will not forget. She is writing it all down.

———

I had one great stab of joy last night. My husband and I had gone to bed. We were almost asleep when I heard the couple we were camping with calling quietly outside our tent. Were we still awake? They had something to show us. . . .

We roused ourselves and unzipped the tent. Zzzzziiiip. My husband was in his underwear and I in my long-john nighty. But these are our oldest friends. They are like family. And so we leaned out of the tent, knees on the grass, and gasped.

Our friend held a huge frog in his fishing net. He shined his flashlight on it and the world stopped. The frog's stomach was pinkish white. This surprised me somehow. One of his long legs dangled out of the net. And oh, his feet! Tiny delicate webs. I put my palm underneath one foot and lifted it up. He blinked his eyes. And eyes! Darkest blue that can still be blue and not be black, rimmed by a gold, flecked color.

And then I saw his fingers. His skinny exact fingers clutched the green net like Hansel's finger sticking out of the cage. I remember blurting out, How could anyone not love God?

This frog was God. He had God all over him, all through him. Made by God. Made by God. I thought I'd never seen such a beautiful thing in my life as this ordinary frog.

And what dignity! He knew who he was. Exactly. And what he was. He let us examine him. The pinkish flesh below his chin throbbed in and out. Even his sliminess reeked of something sacred.

And us! Oh, us! The four of us. Friends. History. Our children asleep in their tents. Us out here ooohing and aaahing over this frog. Shining the light on his tummy. Holding up God in the night. Then goodnight, goodnight. They let the frog go. We all went to sleep.

———

Six months ago, my youngest brother wanted to be a pastor. Last week he called to say he doesn't believe in God anymore. I think he expected me to be shocked. Or to try to talk him back into God.

I wanted to laugh. My brother is blond, with a wide jaw and earnest blue eyes like our father's. I told him good for him. I think this is the right step. Quit church. Have your doubts. Give up on God—if you can.

———

When we get home from camping, the house is stale. No one can breathe. My husband falls asleep in a chair. The boys start fighting. Finally I tell them, Let's drive over to the park. You will play, I will read and write.

But I'm unfit to be seen. I have camping hair, so I put on a baseball cap.

When we get to the park, I find a shady spot. The boys run off and I settle on my tummy on a blanket. And then, since I look like this, I would see someone I know and it would have to be her. She is a woman acquaintance of mine—not just pretty, but modelish-pretty.

She comes over to say hi. Pink shorts. Expensive sunglasses. I tuck my hair into my cap. I shove my notebook farther beneath my chest. We exchange niceties. I can tell she's trying to see me. She wonders about me. And I cannot begin to help her.

———

This book is about me trying to see myself. And you trying to see yourself. This page is a double-sided mirror. And neither of us can really see the other.

———

Nothing I write is totally true. For example, this past minute. You might assume I wrote the above paragraph in one long spasm. You don't see that my oldest son just interrupted to ask for a pop. Or that seconds earlier I yelled at them both to quit squabbling on the swings. The whole truth about any one moment is more than anyone can say at once.

A friend informed me recently that we think at twelve hundred words per minute. But we can only talk at two hundred words per minute. We can write at even less.

———

The other day the phone rang in the middle of my writing. I hoped it would be the man. I prayed it wouldn't be the man. I answered. It was a man, but not the man. This man was from Killer pesticides. They'd be out in my neighborhood soon and would I like a free inspection?

How irritating. Of course he would find bugs, and want to get rid of them! I politely, curtly said, No thank you, sir, I'm not interested, and hung up.

But I couldn't concentrate again after that. I kept

thinking about that phone call. My father had a job doing phone sales once. His master's degree had grown useless and so he called people up. But he only lasted two days. They could probably hear something shaky, pathetic in his voice.

Like this man. His voice had sounded fortyish. Too old to be doing phone sales. His life has gone wrong somewhere. Where? I demand to know. What happened to you?

———

A human being just called me. He got up today and remembered to get dressed. He had coffee. He brushed his teeth, or forgot to, in front of a mirror. But he didn't look at himself much. He avoids his own eyes as he gets ready for work. He has a job doing phone sales.

Maybe the last three numbers he got answering machines. This time he gets a woman's voice. An ordinary housewife. He's glad, until he hears her sigh heavily during his speech. At first pause, she says sharply, No thank you, I'm not interested. Clunk.

And he receives the blow, barely flinching. He is getting used to them. He dials the next number. Can I come search your house for bugs?

———

Today God made me gasp again. But these days, God always makes me gasp. This time it was Miriam and Aaron. They were speaking against Moses, whom God had chosen to lead the Israelites out of Egypt. And they were also saying, Well, hey! Didn't God speak through us, too?

God can't believe it. The gall of them. He calls them both forward and says from a cloud, Who do you think you are? The only person I speak with face to face is Moses. Other prophets have dreams or visions. I only talk face to face with Moses!

When the cloud of God rises from the tent, Miriam is left standing there covered with leprosy, white as snow. Aaron cries out and begs Moses: Oh, forgive our sin! He says, Don't let her be like a stillborn infant from her mother's womb, with her flesh half eaten away!

Moses in turn begs God, Forgive them! Forgive them!

But all God says back to Moses is, What if Miriam's father had spit on her face? Wouldn't she have been in disgrace for seven days? So make her sit outside the camp for seven days.

———

Itsy, bitsy, tiny orange bugs keep landing on my notebook pages and on my arms. I stare at one of them. What a ridiculous bug! How can it exist? It's smaller than the very tip of my pen. But a speck on the page. And yet, when I move my hand to smear it, it jumps away! Fast!

How can such a tiny bug jump so quickly and so far? Where does it get its strength? How stupid you are to write, says the tiny orange dot on my paper back to me. Do you think you can know anything? Can you figure anything out?

———

This book is about hacking legs off, paragraphs, pages even. I go about like an exterminator. One small move, you're dead. If you begin to crawl away from the wall, from this book, at all, I will swipe you off the face of the earth.

———

I stare hard at the grass here at the park. And I think of all we have been through together by now, you and I.

I hope that you are twenty-seven, too. Or else that you are not.

Let's assume I know you. I love you. Let's assume you are the woman on the couch the other night after a writer's meeting. Her children are small. She says she is dying. She has only one small hole poked in her sky, her writing. And she is leaning up to it, trying to breathe, longing to rip it open.

That is what I hope for.

———

The other night I met with that same woman whose children are small at the library. Afterward, we went to a coffee house and talked. I'm trying to help her with writing. But I am also trying to help her with God.

I suggested maybe God isn't as safe or ordinary as people think. I told her what God had done to Miriam. And I pointed out that God hasn't changed since then. He is the same.

She was doubtful. So how does Jesus fit into all this? she wanted to know. What about Jesus?

I said quickly back to her, Thank God for Jesus! Thank God he stands between us and God.

And then she laughed. Good answer! she said. Good answer!

———

Suddenly a huge monstrous insect comes crawling across the blanket for my arm! But no. It only looks that way because I have been staring too long at the orange bug. It is just an ant. I flick it off, send it flying.

———

Here is the proof of Jesus, brother, though there is none. It is not the children playing in the dusk. Or the sacred frog.

Or even the tiny orange smear on this page.

It is the fact that I am not white with leprosy. I unzipped my bag to find my life. Now I stand outside camp, mourning my disgrace, because my father spit on me. I want to know why. And I demand to talk to God face to face.

Part Three
WATCHING OUT FOR GOD

13
The Capture

SOMETIMES I WONDER if I am writing my life, or living it. Or if I do one to do the other. And it occurred to me today that I could keep writing this book forever and never stop.

———

I have a new grandpa now. His name is Orville. I found him in the local newspaper. I was eating my cereal the other morning when I spotted his kind, wrinkled face smiling out at me.

Orville is a farmer, and he's perfect so far as grandpas go. He had on glasses, a straw hat, and a flannel shirt with coveralls. He is proudly holding up a cob of his corn for the photographer. I cut out his picture and pasted it in my notebook. And underneath it I wrote in pen, This is my new grandpa!

———

Every few days I open my notebook to stare at my grandpa's shriveled face, which is extra wrinkled now with the Elmer's school glue I used to paste him in. I say, Grandpa, what will happen? What will happen?

Sometimes I stare into his kind eyes and try hard to imagine he is really my grandpa. And that when I look at him I can feel generations, life, family, blood—love flowing back year upon year upon year. . . .

———

I wonder what my new grandpa would think if he knew some ordinary housewife with children of her own who lived somewhere in town had pasted his picture in her notebook and adopted him for her own grandpa, sight unseen.

I think he would give me some of his corn for free, fresh out of his fields.

———

My new grandpa gives me hope for mankind, and for men in general.

———

I have decided to become an Eskimo, or else I already am one. I have been reading a book about them. At night I go to bed dreaming of ice and floes and seals. And in the morning I wake up and imagine I'm riding across the smooth world on a dog sled.

A few nights ago I read about a very old Eskimo man who reminded me of my new grandpa. I haven't been able to forget about him. What he did. Or what they did to him.

The Eskimo men all go hunting together and are supposed to share what they catch. After one man harpoons an animal, the other men toss their harpoons into it, too. Wherever their weapon lands marks the section of meat that will be their portion.

Once there was a very old Eskimo man who had

gone lame in both his arms. He still went hunting with
the younger men, but he couldn't toss a harpoon. So he'd
fill his mouth with rocks and then spit them at the catch
to mark his portion.

Sometimes the young men would tease the old man.
They would drag the animal too far out on the ice for him
to reach. And then they'd laugh as the old man cried and
wailed and spit his rocks to no avail.

I keep picturing that. This wrinkled old man, his
cheeks bulged out. I keep thinking how the rocks would
feel in his mouth. I imagine his empty stomach grumbling.
The brown lump of seal or walrus on the distant ice. The
sound of male laughter.

———

This morning when I was reading my Bible, a psalm
reminded me of the old Eskimo man again. The psalmist
was saying that his heart and flesh fail him. But God is
his strength and portion forever.

And then I imagined I was a very old man, lame in
both arms. I cried and spit my rocks at God to mark my
portion. And I begged Jesus to bring God closer.

———

This book is not about my father anymore. This book is
about God.

———

Annie Dillard said in an interview once that the hardest
thing to remember is God. She forgets God every day, she
says. Why didn't God make us remember him?

———

Sometimes I can't remember God either. But sometimes I
can't forget him. What he did. Or what they did to him.

———

Yesterday, God made me cry. I was praying an ordinary prayer and talking to him. And then he asked me, Can I trust you? Can I trust you?

I've had God ask me questions before, but they were always for my sake. So I would learn some lesson. But this time, I could sense God was really on edge. He really wanted to know the answer. There was a pleading, desperate quality to his voice.

I didn't know what to say.

———

When I'm writing at my computer, I like to hear the tink, tink, tink of each letter. Some people prefer to hear no sound at all. They like the letters to be borne silently across the white screen.

But I like the tink, tink, tink. It makes every letter declare itself. A furious flowing of tinka-tinka-tinka-tinka means something is happening. Something is happening!

———

The Eskimos compose poetry, too. But they have no way to write it down. So they sing it instead to the beat of drums. They make it up as they go along, but it has to have some rhythm, a beat. So every few lines they will repeat a phrase like, A-ya, a-ya, aye.

When the world is warm it is fun to go up a hill, A-ya, a-ya, aye.

———

The Eskimos in the book I was reading didn't know God. Had never heard of him. But sometimes they would go and sit and be very still. They would spend hours in silence staring out over the ocean. Saying nothing. Seeing nothing. But something was happening.

———

I have Rainier Maria Rilke's poetry in one of my bathrooms right now. He was a famous German poet. I go in
and read some aloud. But I read from the left side of the
page that is in German. I don't know German. So it is like
tink, tink, tink. And it is like A-ya, a-ya, aye. And I can
hear that my voice sounds desperate and pleading.

Maybe God is an Eskimo. Maybe God beats his drum
and makes up the world as he goes along and sings A-ya,
a-ya, aye. Maybe God is a very old man, lame in both
arms. And he spits rocks at us each day and begs: Jesus,
bring them closer! Oh, bring them closer!

———

God remembers everything that happens.

———

When the Eskimos harpoon a walrus, it takes a long time
to haul it onto the beach. The walrus fights and fights
and tries to swim back out to sea. It takes many men to
hold the rope and wait for the walrus to exhaust itself and
give up.

All the other walruses swim away to safety except
for the captured walrus's mate. It will risk its life to come
back toward shore to try to save its partner. It locks tusks
with the caught walrus and tries to pull it to freedom. But
in the end it cannot, and finally the Eskimos drag the dead
animal onto the beach.

Usually, they're so hungry, they dig right in.

———

God and I are in a tug of war. Maybe God is the harpooned
walrus. Or maybe it is I. Who can say what would happen
if God were to let go?

———

Eskimos commit suicide a lot. When life gets heavier than

death, as they say, then it's time to stop life from happening. Usually they hang themselves. Often children hang older parents. Or in a starving family, a mother might hang her hungry children.

Sometimes, before they hang an old parent who is ready to die, they will have a celebration. A party of sorts. But other times, they might not feel ready to let go. And then they will say to the parent, Oh, please, no! We still want to see your face among us!

———

The Eskimos whole existence is mostly about their existence.

———

I haven't written in my journal for the last three days. That's a new record for me this year. I've been trying it as an experiment. To see if I could do it. And to see if things would still happen to me, even if I didn't write them down. And they did.

When I went back to my journal last night, I didn't know what to say. So I said that for the last three days I've just been living. And I still want to see my face among us.

———

My life keeps moving along. Silently. It moves across the white screen, across the smooth world on a dog sled. My life has a rhythm and a beat. It goes tink, tink, tink, and A-ya, a-ya, aye. I make it up as I go along, but all the words are true.

———

It's hard to talk to God when he's desperate and pleading. When he's like a starved old man spitting rocks at his world as it moves farther and farther away. Sometimes I

118

get the feeling that it's me he's crying and wailing about. I start to think I'm the exact portion he's aiming for.

———

The end of the Eskimo book tells how God finally did come to some Eskimos. They heard about a strange man, a great man who had hung on a pole. He'd been nailed to it and died. But now he was alive.

Two curious Eskimos traveled great distances in the snow to find this man. But God wasn't what they thought. Yes, the man had died on a pole and he was alive. But you couldn't see him. Only a lot of people yelling and singing about him while one man banged small pieces of white wood on a big box.

The Eskimos wanted to know more.

14
The Hand

IT IS ALMOST FALL. I get up and live each day much like I lived the days at the start of this book. Except now I notice myself living them. And since my kids have started back to school, the days begin to yawn at seven o'clock at night instead of eight.

———

My oldest son is playing football this year. He is nine, but looks twelve. He is tall like my husband. And when he comes home from football practice, strolling through the front door, I can tell he feels tall, very tall. He is sweaty and keeps trying to talk to me with the plastic mouthpiece still in his mouth.

For goodness sake, I say, take out the mouthpiece when you are trying to talk. And he does. For a second. He's gotten the position he wanted, he says. He's so excited.

But I can't believe he is standing here in front of me like this and so I say, Go take a shower.

My life begins at 6:00 a.m. Day after day I notice the same me keeps coming into this room, coffee in hand, wet hair. She yanks open the blinds and plops down on her couch. She sets her coffee on a chair at her side.

She is always half-sitting up on the couch, feet at one end, back against the other, so she can look out the window at the hills and the sun coming up. Why does she keep coming here like this? She's convinced something will happen.

Today I read from the prophet Isaiah in the Bible. He was a wild man. All I remember from today's reading was one phrase he kept saying over and over. He would tell the people some terrible thing God was going to do to them. Then he'd say, Yet for all this, God's hand is still upraised. His hand is still upraised.

I tried to picture God standing in the sky somewhere over all the people with his huge hand up in the air as if he was about to swat at them, like my husband does at the table when he sees a fly.

My son who plays football comes up to me almost every day, wanting to measure himself against me. To see if he comes any higher on my body. You are still at my eyebrows, I tell him each day. Just like yesterday you were at my eyebrows.

I told God this morning I didn't want to write today. I think we're moving toward the end, I said. And it needs to be good. I see no point in trying to write it, since I don't feel very holy this morning.

I'm not even up to your eyebrows, I said. Not even on tippy-toe.

———

Yesterday I went to my friend's church and talked to her women's group. It felt like church sometimes feels. They called me one of the "ladies," and they announced that after the brunch, and after I spoke, they would offer a craft demonstration. A flower arrangement or a basket or something like that.

I probably didn't talk enough about God. Or about God the way they're used to God being talked about. I imagined I saw lights in about five sets of eyes. Out of thirty. I decided I'd rather talk to writers. And I decided not to tell them I woke up this morning lusting over the man.

———

An overweight woman with reddish hair kept crying during the prayer time. I got the feeling she always cries at these things by the way several woman went over to comfort her automatically, as if they'd done it last week, too. As if she has some problem or sin that won't go away, ever.

Trust God, I pictured them saying to her. Trust God. And then I thought of God in the sky with his hand upraised. And I thought, Watch out! Watch out!

———

It wasn't that I wished these women harm. How I loved them. I really did! How I longed to open up some chamber in their hearts, like a dryer bin, and toss in something that would rattle and clatter until we all woke up again.

———

Last night I got out my journal and climbed into the swing on the back deck. It was that Hour. My husband and son felt it too and so they came out to the back yard. My husband is teaching our oldest son about football plays, and how to get into your stance. They stood in the green grass in the dusk, and my husband kept saying, Arch your back, arch your back. You get down like this. And you have to move fast. You have to be ready. So that as soon as he says hike, you are off. You're gone before they know it.

———

Half the work when you write your life is figuring out what doesn't go in. Half the work is saying, No, not that. Not that either. This doesn't matter. Nor this.

You don't realize how much I don't say of my life. I have left my husband almost wholly out.

———

Sometimes you fall in love with one part of your life. A few paragraphs you have written or moments you spent on a dock. You are so in love with them, you don't want to take them out. But they are messing up the meaning of the whole thing.

After you take it out, it feels like an empty hole. It feels like a hole that will never be filled.

———

People get impatient with people like the woman with the reddish hair. How long will it take you to get over it? Or to get better?

———

When you write, you have to attempt something greater than you can possibly hope to accomplish. That is the only way you can leave a hole, a gap—some chance for a miracle.

———

Life is real. And so when you write, if you follow an experience to wherever it takes you, it will lead you to some meaning. Not that the meaning will make sense. Not at all. But meanings don't have to make sense to be meaningful.

———

Reading Isaiah makes me think of Frederick Buechner. Buechner calls God our Beloved Enemy. He is a great writer whose books spent many months in various bathrooms of my home on various tanks of toilets. He talks about God's love blows. And he leaves huge gaps in his writing.

———

When we were young, my mom and stepdad took us to church sometimes. It seemed like nobody in that church knew God at all, but you could feel him there sometimes. His solemn side. And my favorite part, the only part that really moved me as a child, was the doxology.

The organ would strike the blaring chord. And the congregation always knew what it meant, what was about to happen. We would all stand up and a shiver would rush down the back of my dress when the voices broke out. Praise God from whom all blessings flow. Praise him all creatures here below.

Everyone always sang the last part louder than any other song in the service. Praise him above, ye heavenly host. And the minister would raise both his hands, his black gown sleeves hanging down. Praise Father, Son, and Holy Ghost!

———

Yesterday my youngest son was sitting outside on the curb with a friend. I was on my way for a walk and I stopped by and said, What are you boys doing? But I asked the question as if I were not one of their mothers, as if I had never seen them before and was merely an interested passerby.

We are making weapons! they said, glad for a grownup to impress. And they held them up for me, their eyes squinting into the sun. Popsicle sticks they had shaved down to sharp points by rubbing them on the sidewalk.

Wow! I said. What are you boys going to use them for? And they said, Oh! We are going to go crow hunting! We are going to kill birds with them. Stab them in the chest. And they raised their hands in a jabbing motion for emphasis.

Oh, really? I said, acting very horrified and impressed. You would really do that?

Oh, yes! they gasped, delighted by my reaction. We would, we would! And I could tell they really wished it. And I said, Poor birds! Poor little birds! And then I walked away shaking my head over the matter, and I could feel their wide smiles behind my back, and I knew that they could never.

———

This morning I noticed the sharpened sticks sitting on the stereo speaker. And I noticed they had no sign of blood or guts on them. Praise God from whom all blessings flow! Praise him all creatures here below!

———

I told my friend I walk with that her son wants to kill

birds. And I also told her that today God had his hand upraised, threatening terrible things. And yet his hand was still upraised. And she said maybe that's because he doesn't really want to let it fall. He hates to.

———

My friend knows God.

———

While I was praying this morning, once I glanced up to see the pinkest, thinnest cloud I've ever seen. It was almost a film. I could see right through it to the dark green outline of the hills. I could even see through to the blue sky behind it.

It drifted, even as I watched it, holding my breath. And then it thinned and thinned until it was almost just a pink puff of smoke disappearing into the trees.

———

This is what my life feels like. My son grows up in an instant. A woman still struggles. A boy couldn't kill a bird. A pink cloud passes over. God's hand is still upraised. And I cry, Holy, holy! God is love. Watch out! Watch out!

15
The Child

MY LIFE HAS come down to ten minutes. Ten minutes I spent a month ago with, but not really with, a boy and a dog. And not even my boy or dog. But strangers.

———

Pitch is the dog. He is well-named, black as hot tar. He is fully dog, fully black, fully male, fully alive and panting, and interested in everything. He is perfect so far as dogs go. He knows who he is and how this world works and what can happen.

I met him in a shocking, unexpected way. Our two worlds collided. Violently. Passionately. So that everything and nothing happened. So that there will always be a split in that space of time in the world. A seam or rip as it were.

I'll try to tell you how it happened. Although the moments leading up to those kinds of things are always ordinary. You are never expecting them. In fact, maybe they happen because you're at your most ordinary and imagine you are far from God.

My writing friend who can't recognize her hand and I were on our way to an author-signing party. I'd come from out of state to stay at her house so we could go together. It was my first author-signing for my first book. It was early morning, sunny, and I was in my van following her in her van.

She lives in the woods. She lives where no one else lives. Where high, thick mossy trees line the road and make you think of Red Riding Hood. Suddenly she pulled her van into a small turnout. She rolled down her window and said she'd forgotten the directions to the bookstore. She said wait for me here. I'll be back.

She drove away and left me alone. I turned off the engine and rolled down my window. It was still early enough that the air was cool. I sat there. I waited. I was parked next to the woods on my right. But then I noticed that someone else did live in this forest.

Across the street to my left, set back from the road, was a squarish brown house, a small mobile home, and a barn with a tin roof. In front of these structures were two small fields with barbed fences, separated down the middle by a dusty gravel drive.

I checked my makeup in the rear-view mirror. I re-applied lipstick. I laid my head back on the headrest and breathed deeply. Then I heard something. A voice. Calling. Then silence. Then a voice again. A child's voice calling someone or something.

That's when I saw the dog. He was a black arrow, his eyes focused, coming down the gravel drive toward me. Not running. Not hurried. But trotting. Deliberately, patiently. Without doubts. Then I heard the child again.

And this time I recognized the name being called: "P-i-i-i-itch."

But the voice didn't call the dog like one normally calls a dog. As if one expects the dog to answer or come. That was what threw me. This calling was halfhearted, as if jesting, playing. Pi-u-i-utch . . . trailing up at the end almost in song.

As Pitch reached my van door, I rolled up my window a bit, just to be safe. What if the dog were to leap suddenly and take off my face?

Then I saw the boy. He'd stopped halfway down the gravel drive. He was just visible to me between the bushes and large grass that overhung the path. Yellow pajamas too short in the legs. Bare feet. Yellow hair. Maybe seven or eight. Who knows, maybe nine. He was every child, every age.

I know he saw me. But he didn't acknowledge me at all. Or the fact that I'd caused his dog to come. Instead he set to playing. He bent over, hung his hands to the ground limply and began to swing them, making baboon motions. He turned his body in a circle, sweeping his arms wide, back and forth.

Now and then he'd pause and almost straighten up to call the dog again, as if it were the last thing that mattered, but somehow his child duty. As if, had the dog come, he might have kept calling him anyway.

Pitch ignored the boy without effort. He circled my van. Then he came to the driver's side and stared at me, panting, his shiny black sides heaving. He lifted his head and leaned it against my door just below the window. His thick pink tongue begged politely for my hand to lick. His green eyes saw me as I was.

And then this small, perfect world, which wasn't mine to see anyway, was split apart yet again. Suddenly a window on the mobile home flew open. A woman's head appeared. An ordinary woman. Every woman. Every woman who has had a child. Who has had a dog. Who has had a hard life. Who has slept later than she should.

She seemed to look my way, then her voice darted into the morning, "Pitch!"

The second the sound broke out, the dog went alert and turned about. He trotted obediently across the street and then up the drive. No looking back. Not hurried, but sure. He went home exactly as he had come.

And then slam!

The window shut out the morning again. And just as quickly, instantly, Pitch spun about and trotted patiently toward my van. And the boy resumed his absent calling. Piieeitch . . . ooooh, Piiiuuuutch!

Ten minutes this took. And then it was over. My friend's van came down the road. When I saw it, it shocked me terribly. I've never been so startled to see something so ordinary. I rolled up my window. Pitch went home. I went to an author party. I never recovered.

All that day, and all weekend, and all this last month, I can't explain my life anymore, can't think of who I am anymore—without thinking of Pitch, the boy, the woman, that particular ten minutes.

———

I visited my mother after the author party. My siblings and their kids went to my mother's too so they could see me. My mom and stepdad live in a big log house. I pulled up in their gravel driveway and it happened again: a crash of worlds.

Their wooden gate was covered with children. Eight cousins hanging, playing. Some threw gravel. Some squatted on the ground. I turned off the ignition and stared at them. I saw my face. My sister's face. My brothers' faces. I thought I might cry.

I got out of the van and approached. Some of the kids I hadn't seen in months. A blonde niece whose father doesn't believe in God anymore offered me kisses. A filthy-faced nephew refused me. I told him that's your loss. And here I was willing to kiss that grime. . . .

Even as they kept playing, all of them also paused. Something had changed. An intruder was among them. And yet I knew they could see me, and almost recognize me. Maybe they smelled child on me. Or Pitch.

But they knew I wasn't actually one of them. And so I would only try to get hugs, ask some cute questions, tell them to quit throwing gravel. I did that. Then they let me pass through, and I went in to join the adults.

———

It was good to be with my family without my husband or children. I haven't done that in ten years. My brothers acted like they loved me, even though they aren't sure if we still know each other. Without my husband, I sensed something vital, something I'd forgotten existed between us, return.

It felt almost sacred to be among them. There is a part of me my brothers alone know. My blood will always smell like theirs. Taste like theirs. It is in the air around us. I am still their sister, after all.

But we didn't say it. We gave awkward hugs. We played a game and argued and teased the way we did when we were little. We ate a huge roast beef dinner and all of us adults sat at the same table, squashed together, passing food every other bite.

The kids clamored and whined and talked in the background. The din. Oh the din! It was so loud, I kept stopping. I kept stopping because I couldn't believe how beautiful their music sounded. Like family. Children. Blood.

And seeing! Oh, seeing! The dishes were cobalt blue and painted with country scenes. The yams were deep orange inside when you split them open with the silver fork. Even the juice that got spilled by a baby looked pink and lovely on the white tablecloth.

———

Before I went to bed, I had a good talk with my brother. About God. About life. The older brother, who's more sure about these things, listened to us from across the room.

The younger brother has given up. God doesn't make sense to him anymore. I saw what he meant. And I kept agreeing with him without changing my mind about God. I kept laughing at the rash things he said. And then he'd laugh, too. But he had this earnest expression on his face the whole time.

I think it was this look on his face that caused me to tell him flat out, You are holy. Perhaps you are holier than you have ever been. I hadn't planned on saying that. But it came out of my mouth so true it shocked me. Startled me to the rafters.

You are more real than I have ever seen you, I said.

———

I slept that night in a special room. It is the guest room and I had never been in it alone. I opened the door slowly, sensing it was really me coming into this room. I turned the key-style switch on the old-fashioned lamp and it lit the walls with a gentle glow.

I saw myself put on my nightie and get my notebook and remove all the lacy pillows from the bed so I could climb in. It is that kind of bed and that kind of room. Full of charm and frill and yet aching with a strange depth.

It's the kind of room that could convince me for a moment life is as it should be. Especially the pearly white pitcher and bowl on the night stand. An old-fashioned picture of a young girl that could be me, that feels like it must be me, hangs on the burgundy-wallpapered wall.

The two pine closets built by my brother, the one who doesn't doubt, stand in opposite corners of the room and act optimistic. The bay window with its ruffled curtains and puffy seat begs you to come sit and dream or make up secrets.

The beat-up antique dresser kept talking to me about how some things do survive. How life has meaning. I wrote it all down. I let the back of my head sink into the huge, mushy pillow. I fell asleep thinking how only a good and lovely little girl would be allowed to go to bed in such a room.

––––

My brother thinks God is dead. But only because he has no idea.

He has no idea that God came to me in yellow pajamas today.

He doesn't know that God got up early and ate cereal all alone. That he climbed the cupboards himself to get a bowl. Poured the milk. Dipped the spoon, brought it to his mouth, and felt it going down into his hungry stomach.

After that he forgot to get dressed. He went straight

outside to his world. He is intimate with it. His world smells of him and he smells of it. He is familiar with that particular tree. That exact bush. He spends his days roaming these two fields with his dog, who is separate from him, but the same.

There is no one else nearby to play with. When you are God and alone, you are the only God alive in the world you made. You are the only child. The blades of grass tickle between your toes. Your cereal sloshes in your tummy. The gravel feels cool beneath your bare feet.

A woman in a van pulls up across the street. She turns off the engine and rolls down her window. She is just sitting there. Brown hair. White face. She is on her way to somewhere.

Christ approaches.

16
The Elephant

I WAKE UP TO MY LIFE. And there it is. I'm sitting on my couch in my den, staring at my hands. I notice the exact way my nail polish is chipped on each of my fingernails. I notice the concreteness of things, the green of the green paint on my wall. The exactness of ordinary things.

I hold my soul carefully, sitting here. And I'm gentle with myself. Have mercy, I say. Have mercy on Heather.

———

It took my mother and father three months to consummate their marriage. I was boiling chicken the other day and peeling off the dead skin when that exact line occurred to me. But I could tell it wasn't just a thought I was having, but something I was writing. They're not the same thing at all, and after a while you learn to tell the difference.

———

This week I found out more about how elephants mate. I've been reading *Surrender the Pink* by Carrie Fisher.

It's a novel about a father-deprived daughter who loses her virginity three times and who only loves men who love her in a leaving way. It is a funny, true book.

Between each chapter, she explains the mating habits of different animals. It turns out that the elephants are very polite. They have a long, romantic courtship. And then only at the female's invitation will the male elephant finally make his move.

_____

My father was like the elephant, only different.

_____

Following chapter 4 in Fisher's book, we learn about the snake. The male snake crawls over the female snake, flicking his tongue in and out. But when the time comes to copulate, the snake has a choice to make. For he has not just one penis, but two. Only he doesn't insert them simultaneously.

I told my friend I walk with about the snakes today. I said, There is a God in heaven, after all. She laughed. And then she said, Hey, that's nothing. Don't you know that worms are both male and female? They can do it with anyone they want.

_____

The Eskimos could do it with anyone they wanted to, too—or at least the men could. If they wanted to sleep with a friend's wife, they simply asked that friend to trade wives that night. And it wasn't polite to say no. So an Eskimo woman never knew for sure who would come into her igloo that night.

_____

The last page of Fisher's novel explains the mating habits of some female human beings. It says that given certain

138

circumstances in childhood, the absence of the male parent in particular, the female in her maturity will fixate on unavailable males and yearn for them mournfully until her death.

———

Once, I fell in love with my father. When I was six and we left on the train. Later he sent me a picture of himself from New York. He was wearing a tan trench coat and standing next to a white car. I thought he was the handsomest man alive. I think I knew right then I would yearn for him mournfully until my death.

———

Today my husband came into my den and handed me a shoebox. He said he was unloading stuff from our garage at the town dump when he caught sight of it.

It was a box of letters my friends wrote me the summer I lived with my dad. There was also a letter from my dad that he wrote me before I came to the Bronx. He said he had noticed I had a way with words. He was dreaming he could pull things together so he could send me to college in the East someday. He wanted to be there with help.

———

Today my father showed up in a shoebox with help.

———

This week I've been reading some of Rilke's essays. He wrote once that there's no such thing as real togetherness or union. Not like we dream of it. We're all fundamentally alone, he said. There are only friendly solitudes, waving hello, as it were. Crying out in recognition from time to time.

———

My youngest son came barging into my office just now. He hands me a picture he colored at school. It's of a Ferris wheel that has seats only at the top. There are also a couple of trees. There are always trees in his pictures. Probably more trees have been drawn by kids than anything else.

On the back, he's copied a poem called "Together." He wants me to read it aloud, so I do. "Because we do all things together, all things improve, even the weather. Our daily meat and bread taste better. Trees are greener, rain is wetter."

———

Trees are exact things. That's why children like them. They have firm, brown bark. And green, leafy branches.

The best poems are about exact things. If you live life in general, that will show.

———

Last night I read more of Rilke's poems. My favorite one is called, "Turning Point." It says that seeing someone is not enough. Possessing is not enough. You must learn to love what you see. Train your heart, look inside, he says.

Rilke loved many women. But it turned out he didn't love any of them. He is dead now, buried deep. And when I read his poems aloud, when I cry out to him from nowhere, he doesn't hear me. But I hear him.

First I read the poem in German, and let the meanings wash over me without the words. I cry reverently. Then I go back and read it again in English, and the meanings are twice as deep. And I cry twice as hard.

———

When the Eskimos composed poetry aloud, sometimes

they would do it in pairs. One Eskimo would get up and chant and dance and when he got tired, his friend took over. They'd keep this up for hours sometimes, alternating back and forth, the drums beating wildly, until they were both drenched with sweat.

After this, the two Eskimos were kindred spirits forever. Eternally linked. They would never sing poetry with anyone else for all the rest of their days. They would hunt together, eat together, share their wives, and marry their children to each other.

Last night I should have called a friend. I could have called my friend who can't recognize her hand. Do you want to hear Rilke in German tonight? He is so sorrowful and beautiful, my friend. I know she would have said yes. And we could have become kindred spirits forever. But I went to bed instead.

———

What is happening? That is the question. Not what has happened or what will happen. But what is happening.

———

I've been writing a poem of my own every day. It's a way to remember to keep forgiving myself, and to remember that God does. I make myself write one every day, even if it's night and I'm ready to fall asleep. Since they are usually terrible poems, I get to have mercy over and over.

———

I thought about the man again the other night. How he was like the elephant and my father, only different. Because the man never made his move.

———

Sometimes I think it's like God put a secret about himself in sex. In the male's sex in particular. As if that urgency or

141

intensity says something important about God. As if it's a good thing, after all.

_____

The other day I came out of my house and a little boy about four years old was out there on his bike. I don't know him, but he looked at me as if he wanted to talk. So I called hello to him.

I have a snake! he said to me, as I came walking up. You do? I asked him, noticing his hand was cupped shut. Can I see it? He nodded his head yes. He seemed so excited to show me. He said, It's just a little snake. And I looked in his palm at an ordinary earthworm.

I smiled. Then I broke his heart. Shattered his world. I'm afraid that's not a snake, I said. It's a worm! He looked stunned, confused. As if he'd never heard of a worm. They crawl in the dirt, I said gently. And they look sort of like snakes, but really they are worms.

He didn't answer me. He seemed to sense that whatever a worm was, it wasn't as good as a snake. And then I kept on walking and he watched me go. Like I was a criminal. Or a liar. Or something worse.

_____

The truth is sometimes hard to take.

_____

It's not any man I want. It is God.

_____

This morning after the kids left for school, I didn't come upstairs like I usually do. I turned up the stereo loud. I sat on the rug in the cold sunlight and let the music beat through me. It was a raw, intense song. Feel like making love. Da da dun. Feel like making love to you.

_____

God gave birth to life. And now he's always wanting to do it again and again and again. He wants to make something happen over and over. Create and create. He is relentless, unceasing, urgent.

But God is not like the snake, the elephant, or even a man. God is like the walrus, risking his life to save mine. God is like the Eskimo. Dance! he calls out to me. Dance with me!

I look outside at the trees. Red and leafy and exact. I gaze at my own hand, then at the child's dirty palm, and at God curled up in the center. He is sexless, pink, writhing, and faceless. And I am his mate, blinded by light, like a lost German poet who's learning to love.

17
The Blood

MY HUSBAND CAME in my den this morning. We sat on my couch and talked for a long time. Then I held him with his head on my chest. He drifted in and out of sleep. He was tired from his long week at work.

Once, he woke up and asked me sadly, What does life mean? As if he thought I might know. I said, I don't know. But it means something.

———

When my husband and I were first married, our car broke down on the highway once. We were poor and young and we didn't even have a quarter. We had to call collect for help. Our baby was cold. We sat on the side of the road for five hours, waiting for someone to pick us up.

Back then we were so poor we used to give our blood for ten dollars. It wasn't really our blood we were giving, but our plasma. When you give blood like that, they give it back to you in the end. They take out the liquid parts and return the blood cells and things you need to live.

———

Maybe you should see your life that way. Not just as your life, but as blood. Blood going out and then coming back to you over and over. You bleed and bleed. But in the end you get back what you need to go live, or to go on.

———

I was small back then, too. I forgot to eat sometimes, like I forget to eat now sometimes. And I would have to wear a heavy coat and boots so that I would weigh enough to qualify to give my blood.

———

My husband goes to bed early. And he gets up in the middle of the night when it's still black outside. He drives to work in the dark and he stays there too many hours.

Sometimes we joke about his job. I will ask him, What did you do today? Did you get all those trucks loaded?

And he always says the same thing back. No, he says, I don't load the trucks, remember? I make sure twenty-three other people get the trucks loaded. And then we both laugh—as if it matters. His life is about loading trucks either way.

———

I knew about my husband's dreams before I married him. Once when we were dating, he dreamed I fell down the crack between his waterbed and the wall. When he woke up, he was on his knees straining and straining to pull his bed away from the wall—hysterical because he'd lost me down that crack.

He was still planning to be a big football star back then. He loved music. But he was good at sports, except the coaches scared him. He was that kind of kid, the kind who only want you to say good things to them and not get mad. Each year he decided not to play football. And each year everyone got mad at him until he played.

It was during high school that the dreams started. His mother would hear him stumbling around in his room at night. She'd walk in to find him in a full sweat, squatting on the floor in his underwear in a football stance. Sometimes he would pound on his walls, groping and hammering, trying to find the door to get out of his room.

———

My husband still dreams sometimes. He cries out in the night or laughs. But I have learned over the years how to calm him down or wake him up.

———

My husband got a scholarship to play college football. So we moved to the state we live in. But he hated it. The coaches yelled a lot, he couldn't ever be what they wanted and the dreams got worse. One day he walked off the field in the middle of practice and got dressed and drove away.

After he quit football, he went to a religious college for two terms, until he got so sick of God that even the thought of God made him sick. Now he works for a large brown delivery company that everybody knows, and he makes sure all the packages get on the trucks every day.

———

A couple of months ago my husband and I decided we couldn't find each other anymore. He doesn't know who he is. We said we should split up for a while. We told our families and all of our friends. We lived that way for a month thinking we would do it.

But we ended up being nicer to each other than we've ever been. Every day we'd say, Are you sure about this?

And we kept remembering our lives all at once, things like us lying side by side in a plasma center next to crazy people waiting for the needle and watching our bags slowly fill with blood. And in the end we couldn't do it.

———

Life is a slow remembering who you really are.

———

My husband wants God to do something. He is sort of like my brother who doesn't believe in God anymore, except he does believe. He just hasn't noticed God for a long time. Why doesn't God make something happen? he says to me. Why doesn't he do something?

A few nights ago, my husband went out to get us some Chinese food, and when he came home he said he wanted to die. He said all these horrible things happened to him while he was standing in the restaurant waiting for our food.

There was a poor family there, he said. And a little girl about ten years old who had a cold and a hacking cough. She was fat and had on a dirty yellow shirt that came only part way down her belly. She'd wipe her nose on her arm, he explained, smearing it across, and the shirt would pull up to reveal her starched white stomach, and then she'd start hacking again.

Then a man came through the lobby, he said, who had no legs and was in a wheelchair and looked very hopeless and grimy. Even the cheap gumball machines upset my husband. He noticed they were padlocked to the ground—like anybody would want to steal the gumball machines. It was all so sickening, he said. The whole thing made him sick.

———

My husband wonders what God meant by all this. Isn't it a wretched thing to be human? he asked me. How do you stand it? I thought about that. How, on the one hand, we are made in God's image. But on the other hand—didn't God have to kill his own Son just so he could stand the sight of us?

———

My husband has started to cry. We went to a movie the other night and he cried the last ten minutes. And then last week we got into a fight and we were driving in the car when I saw tears streaming down his cheeks.

That is so good! I wanted to say. Look! You are crying! You are crying! I wanted to throw a party to celebrate, decorate the house, maybe invite all our friends. But instead I said I was sorry and that I hadn't meant to hurt him. I was just hurt myself.

———

I've been realizing God has problems, too. More than we can imagine. But a lot of God's problems are of his own making. Humans, for example. And so he is sort of in love with a lot of his problems, which is part of the problem. He could have had it easy, but he preferred life. He wanted a miracle instead.

———

My husband is at work right now. It's early morning. I look at my clock and think of him, since I'm writing about him. What is he doing? I imagine him with a clipboard in his hand, watching someone work. Or figuring something out. Maybe it's not going well. This truck is too heavy. Or that one is too light. He is hungry, maybe tired. But life goes on.

———

I want to tell my husband something, anything. What can I tell him?

———

Frederick Buechner says God loves us most when we are being our most human.

———

My husband still has dreams sometimes. He loves music and that is what he wants his life to be about. Hold on! I think I hear God say. Hold on!

What can I tell my husband? I hold his head. I cradle it. I stroke his hair. You are getting old, my friend, is all I say. But he laughs. Because we are both the same age. And we are young.

Your hairline is receding more, I point out, tracing it. And you have more crows-feet around your eyes. It was the year my husband was twenty-six, too, I just now realized. And now he is twenty-seven and it shows.

———

I hold my husband's head to my chest. I listen to his breathing. He's bled a lot this last year. Internal injuries. Hemorrhaging inside. He almost lost me down the crack.

Yes, we're in a sick place, I finally whisper to him. It has all gone wrong. But we're not alone. And you will get your blood back again, now that it's begun to flow. God has done something, husband. He became a human being. He was stabbed through. And he qualified himself to give blood in our place.

———

I watch my husband sleeping. I wait patiently for him to wake up again.

18
The Roof

MY YOUNGEST SON can draw stars now. He came to me a week ago and wanted to know how. So I said, You start like a big A, then you jet through the other side, but not too far, then you come straight across, left to right. And from there the way home is obvious.

The most important thing to remember, I told him, is never lift your pen. He caught on quickly. I could tell he was shocked by how quickly he caught on. Pretty soon he was drawing stars like there was no tomorrow.

———

I've been sifting through the shoebox of letters my husband found. It brought back memories of the Bronx, and of the blind black woman.

The first week I was there, it made me nervous to be around her. I'd never been around a black person, much less a blind person. And so every time I passed her in the hall or went into a room where she was I'd say, Hello! So she'd know it was me.

I kept this up until finally one day she told me in a firm voice, Come here. I did. Then she told me to stop saying hello. She said, Honey, I knows who you are, and I knows exactly where you is!

———

My youngest son can already make stars so well that he's bored with them. He came to me last night with a gum wrapper he was drawing on and said, Watch, Mommy. I can make stars with my eyes shut now. I watched. And he did. No problem.

Then he hugged me and said, I'm so glad I had you for a mommy! And I laughed and said, No, honey, I had you. You didn't have me.

———

When does that happen? When do you stop caring if you can draw stars in the dark or hold your breath or not blink?

———

I realized about a month ago that there's a last time everyone skips across a street. And that most people I know have already skipped for the last time and don't know it.

From here on out it will always be walking or running, growing older and buying things at the store or seeing friends or going to work, but never again will life impel them to skip. When I thought of this, the tragedy of it overwhelmed me so that I skipped all the way home from my friend's house.

———

Skipping is a strange thing. Because it means something. Like trains make the sound of leaving. Skipping is the motion of being totally free, childlike, abandoned of self and to self.

But I learned something else about skipping. You

can't fake it. Or make it happen. It must be something that happens to you.

——

I had another revelation this week, too, besides the skipping thing. I realized that I'm a grownup. A woman even! Every day I wake up and the truth of this surprises me all over again.

——

My youngest son is adamant that he wants to be an artist when he grows up. But right now he still draws the flowers bigger than the horse. There's a picture of his like that hanging on the fridge. People always remark on how good the horse is. And my son always wavers, hesitates. Then finally he admits it. He traced the horse.

——

I never heard from the blind black woman again. But in the shoebox I found a letter from another woman who lived in that same halfway house. Finding it made me cry. Her name was Pauline and she wrote me once after I left the Bronx.

Pauline's husband was a recovering heroin addict and she worked at a bank in Manhattan. She had long dark hair and black eyes and she was kind to me.

Sometimes she'd take me shopping, or we would lie out in the sun on the flat, tar roof. We spent hours up there, sweltering in the heat. Trying to get tans. That was what made me cry in the letter. She said, You will have to come visit again someday, and we will go up on the roof. . . .

——

My youngest son is afraid to die. Lately he's had a lot of questions about dying. He isn't worried about his body, though, like my mother was. He's worried about heaven.

He says he doesn't want to go there forever. He wants to stay here.

———

It's strange how you share a piece of your life with someone like that. You lie on a towel and sweat with some woman. You bake together. You turn on the radio. And it is intimate. You feel each other's being, you pass comments about how hot it is, and maybe it's time to turn over.

One woman with an addict husband whose life has gone all wrong. And one girl, a child-woman, lost in her life, in her family. She's used to an ordinary neighborhood and riding her ten-speed bike. They both end up in the same brick halfway house in the Bronx on the same black roof, scorched together forever.

———

How did we all end up on this hot black roof, this flat baking pit?

———

It hurts to feel life. To pause. To stop and listen to your own breathing. But you have to lay yourself open to it all. Because that's where God is. There is no life apart from God, because God is not apart from life. If you turn away, if you run, you will miss both.

———

Once, while I was staying in the Bronx, a man killed himself in the other halfway house across town. It was just like ours, only it had different people. He hung himself in the back yard, and it was the children who found him. It scared us all, because everyone recognized the hopelessness. Most of those people wanted to die, too.

This was no home, no one's home. No one felt at

home there, only they found solace in gathering together in their lostness.

———

Pauline was a searching soul. So I have hope for her now. Do all searching souls find home? If I saw her again, I would say, Thank you. I'm sorry you had to iron everyone's clothes in the heat. That was her job. I can still see her forehead beading with sweat. But she never complained.

I pray for her now. I pray for God to look on Pauline, as if God were not already looking. I pray for God to bless this woman, as if God were not already trying to. I pray for God to notice her, as if God could be distracted.

I pray, and it feels like insanity. I pray for a blind, black woman, and for Pauline on the roof. I pray for all of them in that house, wherever they are now, as if God doesn't know exactly. As if God would have to rouse himself, scan the world, and then say, Aha! I remember now. Some lost people.

———

That's another of God's problems. People are dropping like flies. What fails? Is God not trying, or are they not hearing?

Is nothing going as planned? Or is everything going as planned? Or is God still baking us back on that hot tar roof? Baking Pauline into my mind, my life, so that fourteen years later I might remember her and pray?

———

Lately my mother is remembering things, things she didn't know she knew. A couple weeks ago she remembered the name of the cemetery in New York City where my father's parents are buried. She wished she'd thought of it sooner, since my dad probably could've been buried there.

My brother who doesn't doubt called the cemetery long-distance to check. Sure enough, a woman told him. My grandparents are buried there, two bodies deep. In New York, she explained, they're short on room, so they bury one body twelve feet under, then another six feet under.

She said there's still one plot left that they owned. Any of us four kids could have it if we wanted.

I told my brother to tell her that probably none of us would be rushing to claim it.

———

Everyone in my family wants to live.

———

It's almost the end of the year, and I've gotten to the last book in my Bible. I found some things I can tell my son about heaven. How there won't be any more death, sadness, or pain. And no more darkness. We won't even need the moon or stars or the sun, because God will be our light.

———

My son is afraid of heaven. Only because he doesn't realize that heaven will be home. No one feels at home here, buried two bodies deep.

———

I am like my son. Only I want to draw this world in words instead of pictures. Not exactly as we see it, but a layer deeper. Where the real meanings lie. Where the flowers are bigger than the horse for a reason. Where the stars you manage to draw in the dark matter most.

I draw my life with words, without moving my eye, without lifting my pen. I try not to falter, and I stay as close to the edge as I can get. And then I admit it. That it was already there, what moment or meaning God created beforehand. I only traced it.

———

I'm so glad I had you, says God to me when I'm done. And I'm so glad I had you for a God, I say back to him.

———

It said something else about heaven in Revelation. That we will finally see God face to face. Aha! I cried. Aha!

———

I pray again. I pray for Pauline. But this time I call out to the woman on the roof, and not to God. God is doing all he can from his side of the chasm. I call out to her from our side. Hear me, I pray. Hear me, Pauline!

I'm so glad God had you, I pray. Come into being! Wake up, and hear and see! You are blind to the meanings, but he sees you on the roof. He hears your footsteps fall. He knows where you is, and exactly who you are. And from here the way home is obvious.

Author

Heather Harpham is a freelance writer. *I Went to the Animal Fair* is her second book. She has published dozens of articles in family and parenting magazines and wrote a regular column for a women's magazine for four years.

Heather was born in New Brunswick, New Jersey. She has lived in Oregon for over ten years. She has two children—Noah and Nathan—who at this writing are preteens.